IT TROUBLESHOOTING SKILLS TRAINING

PRACTICAL GUIDE TO IT PROBLEM SOLVING FOR ANALYSTS AND MANAGERS

4 BOOKS IN 1

BOOK 1
FOUNDATIONS OF IT TROUBLESHOOTING: A BEGINNER'S GUIDE

BOOK 2
MASTERING COMMON IT ISSUES: INTERMEDIATE TROUBLESHOOTING TECHNIQUES

BOOK 3
ADVANCED IT PROBLEM-SOLVING STRATEGIES: EXPERT-LEVEL TROUBLESHOOTING

BOOK 4
BEYOND THE BASICS: SPECIALIZED APPROACHES IN IT TROUBLESHOOTING

ROB BOTWRIGHT

Published by Rob Botwright
Library of Congress Cataloging-in-Publication Data
ISBN 978-1-83938-767-8
Cover design by Rizzo

Disclaimer

The contents of this book are based on extensive research and the best available historical sources. However, the author and publisher make no claims, promises, or guarantees about the accuracy, completeness, or adequacy of the information contained herein. The information in this book is provided on an "as is" basis, and the author and publisher disclaim any and all liability for any errors, omissions, or inaccuracies in the information or for any actions taken in reliance on such information. The opinions and views expressed in this book are those of the author and do not necessarily reflect the official policy or position of any organization or individual mentioned in this book. Any reference to specific people, places, or events is intended only to provide historical context and is not intended to defame or malign any group, individual, or entity. The information in this book is intended for educational and entertainment purposes only. It is not intended to be a substitute for professional advice or judgment. Readers are encouraged to conduct their own research and to seek professional advice where appropriate. Every effort has been made to obtain necessary permissions and acknowledgments for all images and other copyrighted material used in this book. Any errors or omissions in this regard are unintentional, and the author and publisher will correct them in future editions.

BOOK 1 - FOUNDATIONS OF IT TROUBLESHOOTING: A BEGINNER'S GUIDE

BOOK 2 - MASTERING COMMON IT ISSUES: INTERMEDIATE TROUBLESHOOTING TECHNIQUES

BOOK 3 - ADVANCED IT PROBLEM-SOLVING STRATEGIES: EXPERT-LEVEL TROUBLESHOOTING

BOOK 4 - BEYOND THE BASICS: SPECIALIZED APPROACHES IN IT TROUBLESHOOTING

Welcome to the "IT Troubleshooting Skills Training" book bundle, a comprehensive resource designed to equip analysts and managers with the essential tools and techniques needed to navigate the intricate world of IT problem-solving. In today's fast-paced and ever-evolving digital landscape, the ability to troubleshoot effectively is paramount for ensuring the smooth operation of IT systems, minimizing downtime, and delivering optimal performance.

This practical guide is tailored to meet the diverse needs and skill levels of IT professionals, from beginners seeking to establish a solid foundation to seasoned experts looking to explore specialized approaches. Spanning four distinct volumes, each book in this bundle offers a progressive learning journey that covers fundamental concepts, intermediate techniques, advanced strategies, and specialized methodologies.

Book 1 - "Foundations of IT Troubleshooting: A Beginner's Guide" lays the groundwork by introducing readers to the core principles and components of IT systems. From understanding hardware and software fundamentals to grasping the basics of troubleshooting methodologies, this book provides a comprehensive overview for those embarking on their IT troubleshooting journey.

Building upon this foundational knowledge, Book 2 - "Mastering Common IT Issues: Intermediate Troubleshooting Techniques" delves deeper into the intricacies of IT troubleshooting. Readers will learn how to identify and resolve a range of common issues encountered in IT environments, from network connectivity problems to software configuration errors, using intermediate-level techniques and best practices.

For those ready to take their skills to the next level, Book 3 - "Advanced IT Problem-Solving Strategies: Expert-Level Troubleshooting" offers an in-depth exploration of advanced methodologies and strategies employed by seasoned IT professionals. From conducting root cause analysis to leveraging diagnostic tools and automation, this book equips readers with the expertise needed to tackle complex challenges with confidence and precision.

Finally, Book 4 - "Beyond the Basics: Specialized Approaches in IT Troubleshooting" pushes the boundaries of traditional troubleshooting by exploring specialized domains and cutting-edge techniques. Whether it's troubleshooting in the cloud, addressing cybersecurity threats, or optimizing performance in data centers, this book provides insights into the latest trends and innovations shaping the future of IT troubleshooting.

Throughout this book bundle, readers will find practical guidance, real-world examples, and actionable insights aimed at empowering them to become proficient and resourceful troubleshooters in their respective fields. Whether you're an aspiring IT analyst or a seasoned manager overseeing complex IT operations, this bundle serves as your comprehensive companion on the journey to mastering IT troubleshooting skills. So, dive in, explore, and elevate your problem-solving prowess with the "IT Troubleshooting Skills Training" book bundle.

BOOK 1
FOUNDATIONS OF IT TROUBLESHOOTING
A BEGINNER'S GUIDE

ROB BOTWRIGHT

Components of a computer system encompass various hardware and software elements that collaborate to execute tasks and process data. At the heart of every computer system lies the central processing unit (CPU), often referred to as the brain of the computer. The CPU interprets and executes instructions from the computer's memory, performing arithmetic, logical, control, and input/output (I/O) operations. It consists of an arithmetic logic unit (ALU), responsible for performing arithmetic and logical operations, and a control unit, which coordinates and manages the execution of instructions. The CPU communicates with other components via the system bus, a communication pathway that allows data and instructions to flow between different parts of the computer. Memory, another crucial component, stores data and instructions temporarily or permanently. Random access memory (RAM) provides temporary storage for data and program instructions that the CPU needs to access quickly. It is volatile, meaning it loses its contents when the computer is powered off. In contrast, read-only memory (ROM) stores firmware and basic input/output system (BIOS) instructions, which remain intact even when the computer is turned off. Storage devices, such as hard disk drives (HDDs), solid-state drives (SSDs), and optical drives, store data persistently, allowing users to save files and programs for future use. HDDs use magnetic storage to store data on spinning disks, while SSDs use flash memory for faster data access and improved reliability. Optical drives, such as CD-ROMs and DVD-ROMs, use lasers to read and write data on optical discs. Input devices enable users to interact with the computer by entering data and commands. Common input devices include keyboards, mice, touchscreens, and microphones. Keyboards allow users to input text and commands, while mice provide a graphical interface for selecting and manipulating objects on the screen. Touchscreens enable direct interaction with graphical user interfaces (GUIs), while microphones capture audio input for voice commands and communication. Output devices display information generated by the computer to users. Monitors, printers, and speakers are examples of output devices. Monitors display visual output, such as text, images, and videos, allowing users to interact with the computer's GUI. Printers produce hard copies of digital documents and images, while speakers output audio for multimedia content and system notifications. Expansion cards enhance the functionality of a computer system by adding new features or capabilities. Common expansion cards include graphics cards, network interface cards (NICs), and sound cards. Graphics cards, also known as video cards or GPUs (graphics processing units), render and display graphics on the computer's monitor. NICs enable wired or wireless connectivity to networks, allowing the computer to communicate with other devices and access the internet. Sound cards process audio signals for playback through speakers or headphones, providing high-quality sound output for multimedia applications and gaming. Finally, the motherboard serves as the main circuit board of the computer, connecting and integrating all other components. It provides electrical connections between the CPU, memory, storage devices, expansion cards, and other peripherals. Additionally, the motherboard contains the BIOS, which initializes the hardware and loads the operating system during the boot process. In summary, the components of a computer system work together seamlessly to perform a wide range of tasks, from simple calculations to complex multimedia processing. Understanding these components is essential for troubleshooting hardware issues, upgrading system performance, and optimizing overall system functionality.

Types of IT systems encompass a broad spectrum of technologies and architectures designed to support various organizational needs and objectives. One common classification categorizes IT systems based on their functionality and scope within an organization. Enterprise resource planning (ERP) systems integrate core business processes, such as finance, human resources, supply chain management, and customer relationship management, into a single unified platform. ERP systems streamline operations, improve efficiency, and provide real-time visibility into organizational activities. Customer relationship management (CRM) systems focus on managing interactions and relationships with customers, prospects, and other stakeholders. CRM systems enable businesses to track customer interactions, manage sales pipelines, and *deliver personalized experiences to customers. Supply chain management (SCM) systems optimize the flow of goods and services from suppliers to customers. SCM systems coordinate procurement, production, inventory management, and distribution processes to minimize costs and maximize efficiency. Human resource management (HRM) systems automate and streamline HR processes, such as recruitment, onboarding, payroll, performance management, and training. HRM systems improve workforce productivity, enhance employee satisfaction, and ensure compliance with labor regulations. Business intelligence (BI) and analytics systems collect, analyze, and visualize data to support decision-making and strategic planning. BI systems provide insights into business performance, market trends, customer behavior, and competitive landscape, empowering organizations to make data-driven decisions. Content management systems (CMS) facilitate the creation, storage, organization, and publishing of digital content, such as documents, images, videos, and web pages. CMS platforms streamline content authoring, collaboration, version control, and workflow management, enabling organizations to create and manage content efficiently. Collaboration and communication systems enable individuals and teams to collaborate, communicate, and share information seamlessly. Collaboration tools, such as email, instant messaging, video conferencing, and document sharing platforms, facilitate teamwork, knowledge sharing, and project collaboration across geographically dispersed teams. Knowledge management systems capture, organize, and distribute knowledge within an organization. Knowledge management systems include repositories, wikis, forums, and expertise locators that enable employees to access and share information, best practices, and lessons learned. Transaction processing systems (TPS) automate and manage routine business transactions, such as sales orders, payments, inventory updates, and customer inquiries. TPS systems ensure the timely and accurate processing of transactions, supporting day-to-day operations and decision-making. Decision support systems (DSS) provide analytical tools and models to support decision-making at various levels of an organization. DSS systems include data analysis, forecasting, simulation, and optimization tools that help managers and executives evaluate alternatives, assess risks, and make informed decisions. Executive information systems (EIS) deliver summarized reports and key performance indicators (KPIs) to senior executives and decision-makers. EIS systems provide a high-level overview of organizational performance, trends, and critical metrics, enabling executives to monitor performance and identify areas for improvement. Geographic information systems (GIS) capture, store, manipulate, analyze, and visualize geographic data to support spatial analysis and decision-making. GIS systems integrate maps, satellite imagery, and demographic data to help organizations solve location-based problems and make location-aware decisions. Healthcare information systems (HIS) manage patient records, medical histories, appointments,* treatments, and billing information within healthcare organizations. HIS systems improve patient care, enhance operational efficiency, and ensure compliance with healthcare regulations. Educational management systems (EMS) support administrative and academic functions within educational institutions, such as student enrollment, course scheduling, grading, and reporting. EMS systems facilitate communication between students, teachers, parents, and administrators, enabling efficient management of educational resources and activities. Financial management systems (FMS) automate and streamline financial processes, such as accounting, budgeting, financial reporting, and asset management. FMS systems provide visibility into financial performance, ensure regulatory compliance, and support strategic financial planning. Manufacturing execution systems (MES) manage and monitor manufacturing processes, including production scheduling, quality control, inventory management, and equipment maintenance. MES systems optimize production efficiency, reduce costs, and improve product quality by coordinating activities on the factory floor. Transportation management systems (TMS) optimize the movement of goods and materials throughout the supply chain, from production facilities to distribution centers to end customers. TMS systems facilitate route planning, freight consolidation, shipment tracking, and carrier management, helping organizations reduce transportation costs and improve delivery performance. Warehouse management systems (WMS) control and optimize warehouse operations, including inventory management, order picking, packing, and shipping. WMS systems improve warehouse efficiency, accuracy, and productivity by automating routine tasks and providing real-time visibility into inventory levels and movements. Document management systems (DMS) organize, store, and retrieve digital documents and files, such as contracts, invoices, and reports. DMS systems manage document lifecycles, enforce security policies, and ensure compliance with regulatory requirements, such as data privacy laws and retention policies. Learning management systems (LMS) deliver and manage online training and educational courses for students, employees, and learners. LMS platforms support course creation, delivery, assessment, and reporting, enabling organizations to deliver effective and scalable training programs. Social media management systems (SMMS) facilitate the management and monitoring of social media accounts and campaigns across multiple platforms. SMMS platforms provide tools for scheduling posts, analyzing engagement, responding to comments, and measuring social media ROI, helping organizations build and maintain their social media presence. Point-of-sale (POS) systems process sales transactions and manage customer payments at retail stores, restaurants, and other businesses. POS systems integrate with inventory management, accounting, and customer relationship management (CRM) systems to provide a seamless retail experience for customers and merchants. Reservation systems automate and manage bookings *and reservations for hotels, airlines, restaurants, event venues, and other businesses. Reservation systems enable customers to book services online, check availability, and receive confirmations, while helping businesses manage capacity and optimize revenue. Legal case management systems (CMS) organize and track legal cases, documents, deadlines, and client communications within law firms and legal departments. CMS systems improve case management efficiency, ensure compliance with legal requirements, and enhance client service by providing centralized access to case information. Property management systems (PMS) automate and streamline property management tasks, such as rent collection, maintenance scheduling, tenant communication, and lease management. PMS systems help property managers and landlords optimize occupancy rates, reduce vacancy periods, and enhance tenant satisfaction. Time and attendance systems (TAS) track and record employee work hours, attendance, and leave requests. TAS systems automate timekeeping, payroll processing, and compliance with labor regulations, helping organizations manage labor costs and ensure accurate payroll calculations. Reservation systems automate and manage bookings and reservations for hotels, airlines, restaurants, event venues, and other businesses. Reservation systems enable customers to book services online, check availability, and receive confirmations, while helping businesses manage capacity and optimize revenue. Legal case management systems (CMS) organize and track legal cases, documents, deadlines, and client communications within law firms and legal departments. CMS systems improve case management efficiency, ensure compliance with legal requirements, and enhance client service by providing centralized access to case information. Property management systems (PMS) automate and streamline property management tasks, such as rent collection, maintenance scheduling, tenant communication, and lease management. PMS systems help property managers and landlords optimize occupancy rates, reduce vacancy periods, and enhance tenant satisfaction. Time and attendance systems (TAS) track and record employee work hours, attendance, and leave requests. TAS systems automate timekeeping, payroll processing, and compliance with labor regulations, helping organizations manage labor costs and ensure accurate payroll calculations.*

The troubleshooting process is a systematic approach used to identify, diagnose, and resolve technical problems in various systems, ranging from computers and networks to machinery and equipment. It involves a series of steps designed to isolate the root cause of the issue and implement corrective actions to restore normal functionality. The process typically begins with gathering information about the problem, including its symptoms, impact on operations, and any recent changes or events that may have triggered it. This initial step helps to define the scope of the problem and guide subsequent troubleshooting efforts. Once the problem is defined, the next step is to identify possible causes or hypotheses that could explain the observed symptoms. This may involve reviewing system configurations, logs, error messages, and other relevant data to pinpoint potential sources of the issue. In some cases, troubleshooting guides, manuals, or online resources may be consulted to explore common causes and solutions for similar problems. After generating hypotheses, the troubleshooter then conducts tests or experiments to validate or eliminate each potential cause systematically. This may include performing diagnostic tests, running troubleshooting tools, or conducting controlled experiments to isolate the problem. During this phase, it is essential to document the steps taken, observations made, and results obtained to facilitate collaboration and knowledge sharing with other stakeholders. As the troubleshooting process progresses, the troubleshooter narrows down the list of possible causes based on the test results and observations. This may involve iterating through the previous steps multiple times to refine hypotheses and gather additional evidence to support or refute them. In some cases, the troubleshooter may need to consult with colleagues, experts, or vendors for assistance in troubleshooting complex or unfamiliar issues. Collaboration can provide valuable insights, alternative perspectives, and access to specialized knowledge or resources that may help expedite the resolution process. Once the root cause of the problem is identified, the troubleshooter develops and implements a plan to address it effectively. This may involve applying known solutions, making configuration changes, installing patches or updates, replacing faulty components, or implementing workarounds to mitigate the issue temporarily. Care should be taken to consider the potential impact of proposed solutions on system stability, performance, and security to minimize unintended consequences. After implementing the corrective actions, the troubleshooter verifies that the problem has been resolved by testing the system to ensure that it functions as expected. This may involve performing functional tests, monitoring system performance, and soliciting feedback from end-users to confirm that the issue has been addressed satisfactorily. If the problem persists or reoccurs despite the corrective actions taken, the troubleshooter may need to revisit earlier steps in the troubleshooting process to reassess assumptions, gather additional information, or explore alternative hypotheses. Troubleshooting is an iterative and dynamic process that requires patience, persistence, and problem-solving skills to achieve successful outcomes. It often involves a combination of technical expertise, critical thinking, and creativity to navigate complex problems and arrive at effective solutions. Moreover, effective communication and collaboration are essential for sharing knowledge, coordinating efforts, and leveraging collective expertise to resolve challenging issues collaboratively. By following a structured troubleshooting process and leveraging best practices, troubleshooters can effectively diagnose and resolve technical problems, minimize downtime, and optimize system performance and reliability. The importance of a methodical approach cannot be overstated when it comes to problem-solving, decision-making, and achieving goals effectively. A methodical approach involves following a systematic and organized process to analyze, plan, and execute tasks or solve problems in a logical and structured manner. This approach helps to ensure that all relevant factors are considered, potential risks are identified and mitigated, and optimal solutions are implemented efficiently. One of the key benefits of a methodical approach is that it helps to reduce uncertainty and ambiguity by providing a clear framework for action. By breaking down complex tasks or problems into smaller, manageable steps, individuals can gain a better understanding of the problem space, identify dependencies and interrelationships, and develop a roadmap for achieving their objectives. Additionally, a methodical approach enables individuals to prioritize tasks effectively and allocate resources efficiently based on their relative importance and urgency. This ensures that limited time, energy, and resources are invested in activities that yield the greatest value and contribute to the achievement of overarching goals. Another advantage of a methodical approach is that it fosters consistency and repeatability in decision-making and problem-solving processes. By establishing standardized procedures, criteria, and metrics for evaluating options and making choices, individuals can make more informed and consistent decisions across different contexts and scenarios. This consistency not only reduces the likelihood of errors and oversights but also enhances accountability and transparency by providing a clear rationale for decisions made. Furthermore, a methodical approach promotes collaboration and teamwork by providing a common framework and language for communication and coordination among team members. By documenting processes, sharing best practices, and leveraging collective expertise, teams can collaborate more effectively, avoid duplication of effort, and capitalize on synergies to achieve shared goals. Moreover, a methodical approach enables individuals and organizations to adapt and respond to change more effectively by providing a structured framework for managing uncertainty and complexity. By continuously monitoring progress, evaluating outcomes, and adjusting strategies as needed, individuals can adapt to changing circumstances, seize new opportunities, and overcome unexpected challenges more resiliently. Additionally, a methodical approach facilitates continuous improvement by fostering a culture of learning, reflection, and innovation. By systematically collecting feedback, analyzing performance data, and identifying areas for improvement, individuals and organizations can identify opportunities to enhance efficiency, effectiveness, and quality over time. This iterative process of improvement enables individuals and organizations to stay competitive, responsive, and adaptable in a rapidly changing environment. In summary, the importance of a methodical approach lies in its ability to enhance clarity, consistency, collaboration, adaptability, and continuous improvement in problem-solving, decision-making, and goal achievement. By following a systematic and organized process, individuals and organizations can navigate complexity, manage uncertainty, and achieve better outcomes more reliably. Whether tackling complex problems, making critical decisions, or pursuing ambitious goals, a methodical approach provides a valuable framework for success in any endeavor.

Networking protocols and standards play a fundamental role in enabling communication and interoperability between devices and systems in computer networks. A networking protocol is a set of rules and conventions that govern the format, timing, sequencing, and error control of data exchange between devices on a network. These protocols define how data is transmitted, routed, and received across the network, ensuring reliable and efficient communication. Networking standards, on the other hand, are specifications developed by standards organizations, such as the Institute of Electrical and Electronics Engineers (IEEE) and the International Organization for Standardization (ISO), to ensure compatibility and interoperability between different networking technologies and devices. These standards define the physical, data link, network, transport, and application layers of the network stack, providing a common framework for implementing networking protocols and building network infrastructure. One of the most widely used networking protocols is the Transmission Control Protocol/Internet Protocol (TCP/IP), which forms the foundation of the Internet and many other computer networks. TCP/IP is a suite of protocols that enables end-to-end communication between devices connected to the Internet, providing reliable, connection-oriented communication over IP networks. The Internet Protocol (IP) is responsible for addressing and routing packets of data across the Internet, while TCP ensures that data is delivered reliably and in the correct order by providing error detection, retransmission, and flow control mechanisms. Another important networking protocol is the Hypertext Transfer Protocol (HTTP), which is used for transmitting and receiving hypertext documents on the World Wide Web. HTTP defines how web browsers and web servers communicate, allowing users to access and retrieve web pages, images, videos, and other resources from remote servers over the Internet. HTTPS (HTTP Secure) is a secure version of HTTP that encrypts data transmitted between the client and server using Transport Layer Security (TLS) or Secure Sockets Layer (SSL) encryption protocols, providing confidentiality, integrity, and authentication for web transactions. The Domain Name System (DNS) is another essential networking protocol that translates human-readable domain names, such as www.example.com, into numerical IP addresses, which are used to identify and locate devices on the Internet. DNS enables users to access websites and services using easy-to-remember domain names, rather than complex IP addresses, making the Internet more user-friendly and accessible. Other important networking protocols include the Simple Mail Transfer Protocol (SMTP) for sending and receiving email, the File Transfer Protocol (FTP) for transferring files between computers, the Internet Message Access Protocol (IMAP) and Post Office Protocol (POP) for accessing email messages from a mail server, and the Dynamic Host Configuration

Protocol (DHCP) for automatically assigning IP addresses and other network configuration parameters to devices on a network. In addition to these widely used protocols, there are many other networking protocols and standards that define specific functionalities and services within computer networks. For example, the Ethernet protocol is used for wired LANs, while Wi-Fi (IEEE 802.11) is used for wireless LANs. The IEEE 802.3 standard specifies the physical and data link layer protocols for Ethernet networks, while the IEEE 802.11 standard defines the protocols for wireless LANs. Similarly, the IEEE 802.1X standard specifies protocols for port-based network access control, while the IEEE 802.15 standard defines protocols for wireless personal area networks (WPANs). Other notable networking standards include the Open Systems Interconnection (OSI) model, which defines a conceptual framework for understanding and implementing network protocols, and the Internet Engineering Task Force (IETF) standards, which specify protocols and technologies for the Internet. In summary, networking protocols and standards are essential building blocks of computer networks, providing the rules, conventions, and specifications necessary for devices to communicate and interoperate effectively. By adhering to common protocols and standards, network devices can communicate seamlessly, ensuring compatibility, reliability, and interoperability across heterogeneous networks.

Network topologies and devices form the backbone of modern communication systems, enabling the exchange of data and information between devices in a network. A network topology refers to the physical or logical arrangement of devices, connections, and communication paths in a network. There are several common network topologies, each with its own advantages, disadvantages, and use cases. One of the simplest network topologies is the bus topology, in which all devices are connected to a single shared communication medium, such as a coaxial cable or twisted pair cable. In a bus topology, data is transmitted sequentially along the bus, and each device listens for data addressed to it. While bus topologies are easy to implement and require minimal cabling, they can suffer from performance degradation and data collisions as the number of devices on the bus increases. Another common network topology is the star topology, in which each device is connected to a central hub or switch. In a star topology, data is transmitted directly between devices and the central hub, eliminating the risk of collisions and improving network performance. However, star topologies require more cabling than bus topologies and can be more expensive to implement. A variation of the star topology is the extended star topology, in which multiple star topologies are interconnected using a central backbone cable or switch. This allows for greater scalability and flexibility in larger networks. Yet another network topology is the ring topology, in which devices are connected in a closed loop or ring configuration. In a ring topology, data is transmitted sequentially from one device to the next until it reaches its destination. While ring topologies can provide high-speed, fault-tolerant communication, they can be difficult to troubleshoot and expand due to their closed-loop structure. Mesh topologies are characterized by multiple interconnections between devices, providing redundant paths for data transmission and enhancing network reliability and fault tolerance. Mesh topologies can be fully meshed, in which every device is connected to every other device, or partially meshed, in which only selected devices are interconnected. While mesh topologies offer high reliability and fault tolerance, they can be complex to design and expensive to implement due to the large number of connections required. Hybrid topologies combine two or more of the aforementioned topologies to create a customized network configuration that meets specific requirements and objectives. For example, a hybrid topology may combine elements of a star topology with elements of a mesh topology to create a highly reliable and scalable network. In addition to network topologies, various devices play critical roles in facilitating communication and data exchange within networks. Network devices can be categorized into several broad categories, including network infrastructure devices, network connectivity devices, and network security devices. Network infrastructure devices include routers, switches, hubs, and bridges, which are responsible for routing, switching, and forwarding data between devices on a network. Routers are network devices that connect multiple networks and forward data packets between them based on their destination IP addresses. Switches are network devices that connect *multiple devices within a local area network (LAN) and forward data packets between them based on their destination MAC addresses. Hubs are simple network devices that connect multiple devices within a LAN and broadcast data packets to all connected devices. Bridges are network devices that connect multiple LAN segments and forward data packets between them based on their destination MAC addresses. Network connectivity devices include network interface cards (NICs), modems, and wireless access points (APs), which enable devices to connect to networks and access network resources. NICs are hardware devices that provide network connectivity to computers and other devices by connecting them to a network medium, such as Ethernet or Wi-Fi. Modems are devices that modulate and demodulate digital data to enable communication over analog telephone lines or digital subscriber lines (DSL). Wireless APs are devices that provide wireless connectivity to devices within a local area network (LAN) by transmitting and receiving data over radio waves. Network security devices include firewalls, intrusion detection systems (IDSs), and virtual private network (VPN) gateways, which protect networks from unauthorized access, attacks, and data breaches. Firewalls are devices or software programs that monitor and filter incoming and outgoing network traffic based on predefined security rules and policies. IDSs are devices or software programs that monitor network traffic for suspicious activity and alert administrators to potential security threats. VPN gateways are devices or software programs that establish secure encrypted connections between remote users or networks and a corporate network over the Internet, ensuring privacy and confidentiality of data transmitted over public networks. In summary, network topologies and devices are essential components of modern communication systems, providing the infrastructure and tools necessary for devices to connect, communicate, and exchange data within networks. By understanding the different types of network topologies and devices available, network administrators and engineers can design, implement, and maintain robust, scalable, and secure networks that meet the needs and objectives of their organizations.*

Common hardware failures can disrupt operations, compromise data integrity, and lead to costly downtime for individuals and organizations. Understanding the causes, symptoms, and remedies for common hardware failures is essential for maintaining reliable and efficient computer systems. One of the most common hardware failures is hard disk drive (HDD) failure, which can result from mechanical issues, such as head crashes, spindle motor failure, or disk platter damage. Symptoms of HDD failure include slow performance, unusual noises, system crashes, and data corruption. To prevent data loss due to HDD failure, it is important to regularly back up important files and replace failing drives promptly. Another common hardware failure is random access memory (RAM) failure, which can occur due to overheating, electrical surges, or manufacturing defects. Symptoms of RAM failure include system crashes, blue screen errors, and application instability. To diagnose RAM failures, users can run memory diagnostic tools, such as MemTest86, and replace faulty modules as needed. Central processing unit (CPU) failure is another common hardware issue, which can result from overheating, voltage spikes, or manufacturing defects. Symptoms of CPU failure include system crashes, overheating, and inability to boot. To prevent CPU failure, users should ensure proper cooling and ventilation, avoid overclocking, and monitor CPU temperatures regularly. Graphics processing unit (GPU) failure is also common, especially in gaming and high-performance computing systems. GPU failure can occur due to overheating, voltage spikes, or solder joint fatigue. Symptoms of GPU failure include graphical artifacts, screen flickering, and system crashes during graphics-intensive tasks. To prevent GPU failure, users should ensure proper cooling and ventilation, avoid overclocking, and monitor GPU temperatures regularly. Another common hardware failure is power supply unit (PSU) failure, which can occur due to electrical surges, capacitor aging, or overloading. Symptoms of PSU failure include system instability, random reboots, and unusual noises from the power supply unit. To prevent PSU failure, users should use high-quality power supplies with sufficient wattage and surge protection, and replace aging PSUs before they fail. Motherboard failure is also common, particularly in systems subjected to electrical surges, overheating, or physical damage. Symptoms of motherboard failure include system crashes, device recognition issues, and inability to boot. To prevent motherboard failure, users should use surge protectors, ensure proper cooling and ventilation, and handle components carefully during installation and maintenance. Another common hardware failure is solid-state drive (SSD) failure, which can occur due to wear leveling, firmware bugs, or electronic component failure. Symptoms of SSD failure include slow performance, data corruption, and inability to boot. To prevent SSD failure, users should avoid excessive write operations, install firmware updates regularly, and replace aging SSDs before they fail. Optical drive failure is also common, particularly in systems subjected to dust, debris, or mechanical wear. Symptoms of optical drive failure include read/write errors, disc recognition issues, and unusual noises from the drive. To prevent optical drive failure, users should clean discs and drive optics regularly, avoid using damaged discs, and handle discs carefully during insertion and removal. Network interface card (NIC) failure is another common hardware issue, which can occur due to electrical surges, driver issues, or physical damage. Symptoms of NIC failure include network connectivity issues, slow performance, and device recognition errors. To prevent NIC failure, users should use surge protectors, install updated drivers regularly, and handle NICs carefully during installation and maintenance. In summary, common hardware failures can disrupt operations, compromise data integrity, and lead to costly downtime for individuals and organizations. By understanding the causes, symptoms, and remedies for common hardware failures, users can take proactive steps to prevent hardware failures and ensure the reliability and efficiency of their computer systems. Regular maintenance, proper handling, and timely replacement of aging components are essential for minimizing the risk of hardware failures and maximizing the lifespan of computer hardware.

Diagnosing hardware problems is a crucial skill for computer users and IT professionals alike, as it enables them to identify and resolve issues that may be affecting the performance or functionality of computer hardware.

The process of diagnosing hardware problems involves a systematic approach to troubleshooting, which includes identifying symptoms, gathering information, performing tests, and analyzing results to determine the root cause of the problem. One of the first steps in diagnosing hardware problems is to identify and document the symptoms experienced by the user or observed in the computer system. Symptoms may include error messages, system crashes, slow performance, hardware malfunctions, or unusual behavior. By carefully observing and documenting symptoms, users can provide valuable information that can help narrow down the possible causes of the problem. Once symptoms are identified, the next step in diagnosing hardware problems is to gather information about the affected hardware components and the system configuration. This may involve reviewing system specifications, hardware documentation, and diagnostic tools to identify the make, model, and specifications of the hardware components installed in the computer system. Additionally, users may need to check for firmware updates, driver versions, and system settings that may be relevant to the problem. With the relevant information gathered, the next step in diagnosing hardware problems is to perform tests and experiments to isolate the root cause of the problem. This may involve running diagnostic tests, hardware stress tests, benchmarking tools, or diagnostic utilities to identify hardware failures, compatibility issues, or performance bottlenecks. Users can also try swapping out suspect components with known-good replacements to see if the problem persists, which can help confirm or rule out specific hardware components as the cause of the problem. As tests are performed and data is collected, users should carefully analyze the results to identify patterns, trends, or anomalies that may indicate the root cause of the problem. This may involve reviewing error logs, diagnostic reports, performance metrics, or test results to identify correlations between symptoms and potential causes. Additionally, users may need to consult technical documentation, online resources, or expert forums for guidance on interpreting test results and troubleshooting steps. Once the root cause of the problem has been identified, the final step in diagnosing hardware problems is to implement appropriate solutions to resolve the issue. This may involve repairing or replacing faulty hardware components, updating firmware or drivers, adjusting system settings, or performing maintenance tasks to improve system reliability and performance. Users should carefully follow manufacturer guidelines and best practices when implementing solutions to ensure that they are effective and do not inadvertently cause further damage to the system. Additionally, users should test the system after implementing solutions to verify that the problem has been resolved and that the system is functioning as expected. In summary, diagnosing hardware problems is an essential skill for computer users and IT professionals, as it enables them to identify and resolve issues that may be affecting the performance or functionality of computer hardware. By following a systematic approach to troubleshooting, including identifying symptoms, gathering information, performing tests, and analyzing results, users can effectively diagnose hardware problems and implement appropriate solutions to resolve them. With the right knowledge, tools, and techniques, users can ensure the reliability and performance of their computer hardware and minimize downtime and disruption caused by hardware failures.

Operating system architecture refers to the structure and design principles that govern the organization and operation of an operating system. It defines how various components of the operating system interact with each other and with hardware, applications, and users to provide essential services and manage system resources efficiently. Understanding operating system architecture is essential for developers, system administrators, and IT professionals, as it enables them to design, implement, and manage operating systems effectively. At its core, operating system architecture consists of several key components, including the kernel, system libraries, device drivers, user interface, and system utilities. The kernel is the core component of the operating system responsible for managing system resources, such as memory, processes, files, and input/output (I/O) devices. It provides essential services, such as process scheduling, memory management, file system management, and device drivers, to enable applications to run and interact with hardware effectively. The kernel operates in privileged mode, with unrestricted access to hardware resources, and serves as an intermediary between applications and hardware, providing a unified interface for accessing system resources. System libraries are collections of reusable code modules and functions that provide common services and functionality to applications, such as input/output operations, file manipulation, and networking. They abstract low-level hardware details and provide high-level interfaces for interacting with system resources, making it easier for developers to write portable and efficient applications that can run on different operating systems. Device drivers are software components that enable communication between the operating system and hardware devices, such as disk drives, network adapters, and graphics cards. They provide a standardized interface for accessing device functionality and manage device-specific operations, such as initialization, data transfer, and error handling, to ensure compatibility and reliability across different hardware platforms. User interfaces are components of the operating system that enable users to interact with the system and applications effectively. They provide graphical or command-line interfaces for performing common tasks, such as file management, application launching, and system configuration, and facilitate communication between users and the underlying operating system. User interfaces may include graphical user interfaces (GUIs), command-line interfaces (CLIs), or web-based interfaces, depending on the type of operating system and user preferences. System utilities are software tools and applications bundled with the operating system that provide additional functionality and services to users and administrators. They include tools for system monitoring, performance analysis, troubleshooting, security management, and software installation, among others, and help users manage and maintain their *systems efficiently. Operating system architecture can vary significantly depending on the type of operating system and its intended use case. For example, desktop operating systems, such as Microsoft Windows, macOS, and Linux, typically feature a graphical user interface (GUI) and support for multitasking, multimedia, and networking, to meet the needs of individual users and businesses. Server operating systems, such as Windows Server, Linux, and UNIX, are optimized for running server applications and providing essential services, such as file sharing, web hosting, and database management, in a networked environment. Embedded operating systems, such as Android, iOS, and embedded Linux, are designed for use in resource-constrained devices, such as smartphones, tablets, and IoT devices, and prioritize low power consumption, small footprint, and real-time performance. Real-time operating systems (RTOS), such as FreeRTOS, QNX, and VxWorks, are designed for use in embedded systems and critical applications, such as industrial automation, automotive systems, and aerospace systems, and prioritize deterministic behavior, low latency, and high reliability. Regardless of the type of operating system, all operating systems share common architectural principles and components, such as the kernel, system libraries, device drivers, user interface, and system utilities, which enable them to provide essential services and manage system resources effectively. In summary, operating system architecture is the foundation of modern computing systems, providing the structure and design principles that govern the operation of operating systems. By understanding* operating system architecture, developers, system administrators, and IT professionals can design, implement, and manage operating systems effectively, ensuring compatibility, reliability, and performance across different hardware platforms and use cases. Common operating system errors can disrupt productivity, compromise system stability, and lead to data loss for individuals and organizations. Understanding the causes, symptoms, and solutions for common operating system errors is essential for troubleshooting and resolving issues effectively. One of the most common operating system errors is the Blue Screen of Death (BSOD), which occurs when the operating system encounters a critical error that it cannot recover from, resulting in a system crash and display of a blue screen with error codes and diagnostic information. BSOD errors can be caused by hardware failures, driver issues, software conflicts, or corrupt system files. To resolve BSOD errors, users can try updating device drivers, uninstalling recently installed software or hardware, running system diagnostics, or performing a system restore to a previous stable state. Another common operating system error is the "Operating System Not Found" error, which occurs when the computer is unable to locate the operating system files required to boot the system. This error can be caused by corrupt or missing boot files, damaged hard disk drives, or incorrect BIOS settings. To resolve this error, users can try repairing the Master Boot Record (MBR), rebuilding the Boot Configuration Data (BCD), checking for loose or faulty connections, or reinstalling *the operating system from a bootable installation media. File system errors are another common issue that can occur on operating systems, resulting in data corruption, file loss, or system instability. File system errors can be caused by improper shutdowns, power outages, disk errors, or software bugs. To resolve file system errors, users can run the built-in disk checking utility, such as CHKDSK on Windows or FSCK on Linux, to scan and repair disk errors, recover lost data, and restore file system integrity. Another common operating system error is the "Application Not Responding" error, which occurs when a software application becomes unresponsive and fails to respond to user input or system commands. This error can be caused by software bugs, memory leaks, resource exhaustion, or system overload. To resolve this error, users can try closing the unresponsive application using the Task Manager or Activity Monitor, restarting the computer, or updating the application to the latest version. Network connectivity issues are also common on operating systems, resulting in inability to connect to the internet, access network resources, or communicate with other devices on the network. Network connectivity issues can be caused by misconfigured network settings, faulty network hardware, or software conflicts. To resolve network connectivity issues, users can try restarting the network router and modem, checking network cables and connections, resetting network settings, or updating network drivers. Another common operating system error is the "Low Disk Space" error, which occurs when the computer's hard disk drive is running out of available disk space. This error can be caused by accumulation of temporary files, large file downloads, or excessive usage of disk space by applications and system files. To resolve this error, users can try deleting unnecessary files and applications, emptying the Recycle Bin or Trash, running disk cleanup utilities, or adding additional storage space to the computer. System slowdowns and performance issues are also common on operating systems, resulting in sluggish performance, unresponsive applications, and slow boot times. System slowdowns can be caused by malware infections, disk fragmentation, memory leaks, or outdated hardware. To resolve system slowdowns, users can try running antivirus scans to remove malware, defragmenting the hard disk drive, closing unnecessary background processes and applications, upgrading hardware components, or reinstalling the operating system for a fresh start. In summary, common operating system errors can disrupt productivity, compromise system stability, and lead to data loss for individuals and organizations. By understanding the causes, symptoms, and solutions for common operating system errors, users can troubleshoot and resolve issues effectively, ensuring the reliability and performance of their computer systems. Regular maintenance, updates, and backups are essential for preventing and mitigating operating system errors and minimizing downtime and disruption caused by system failures.*

Software installation methods encompass various techniques and processes used to deploy software applications on computer systems. Understanding different installation methods is crucial for system administrators, IT professionals, and users, as it allows them to install, configure, and manage software efficiently. One of the most common software installation methods is manual installation, where users manually download software installation packages from the internet or install them from physical media, such as CDs or DVDs, and follow step-by-step instructions provided by the software vendor to complete the installation process. Manual installation gives users full control over the installation process and allows them to customize installation options, such as installation directory, components, and settings, to suit their preferences and requirements. However, manual installation can be time-consuming, error-prone, and may require technical expertise to troubleshoot installation issues. Another common software installation method is automated installation, where software installation packages are deployed and installed automatically using specialized deployment tools, such as Microsoft System Center Configuration Manager (SCCM), Windows Deployment Services (WDS), or Group Policy Object (GPO) in a corporate environment. Automated installation streamlines the deployment process, reduces human errors, and ensures consistency and standardization across multiple computers and environments. It also allows administrators to remotely deploy software to large numbers of computers simultaneously, saving time and effort compared to manual installation methods. However, automated installation requires careful planning, configuration, and testing to ensure compatibility, reliability, and security, and may require additional infrastructure and resources to implement effectively. Another software installation method is network installation, where software installation packages are stored on a central network server, and users install software over the network using a network-based installation tool, such as Windows Installer (MSI) or Red Hat Package Manager (RPM). Network installation allows users to install software from a centralized location without the need for physical media or manual intervention, making it ideal for large organizations with multiple users and computers. It also facilitates centralized management, version control, and updates, as administrators can easily deploy, monitor, and update software installations from a central location. However, network installation may require sufficient network bandwidth and infrastructure to support simultaneous installations and may be slower than local installations, especially for large software packages or over congested networks. Another software installation method is cloud-based installation, where software applications are deployed and installed from cloud-based repositories or app stores using web browsers or dedicated software installation tools. Cloud-based installation offers the convenience of on-demand access to a wide range of software applications without the need for physical media or local storage, making it ideal for users who require flexibility, scalability, and mobility. It also allows for automatic updates, license management, and usage tracking, as software vendors can push updates and monitor usage centrally. However, cloud-based installation may raise concerns about data privacy, security, and reliability, as users rely on third-party cloud providers to host and deliver software applications over the internet. Another software installation method is containerized installation, where software applications are packaged with all their dependencies into lightweight, portable containers using containerization technologies, such as Docker or Kubernetes, and deployed and run on any compatible host system. Containerized installation simplifies software deployment, reduces conflicts between dependencies, and enhances system isolation and security, as each container runs in its own isolated environment with its own filesystem, networking, and runtime resources. It also enables developers to build, test, and deploy applications more quickly and consistently across different environments, such as development, testing, and production, by encapsulating application code, dependencies, and configuration into self-contained units. However, containerized installation may require additional overhead and expertise to set up and manage container infrastructure and may not be suitable for all types of applications or environments. In summary, software installation methods encompass various techniques and processes used to deploy software applications on computer systems. By understanding different installation methods, users can choose the most appropriate method for their needs and preferences, whether it's manual installation for individual users, automated installation for large-scale deployments, network installation for centralized management, cloud-based installation for flexibility and scalability, or containerized installation for enhanced portability and security. Regardless of the method chosen, careful planning, testing, and monitoring are essential to ensure successful software installations and optimal performance of computer systems. Troubleshooting software configuration issues is an essential skill for IT professionals, system administrators, and users alike, as it allows them to identify and resolve problems that may arise due to misconfigured software settings, preferences, or options. Software configuration issues can manifest in various ways, such as application crashes, performance degradation, functionality limitations, or unexpected behavior, and may affect individual applications, operating systems, or entire computer systems. Understanding the causes, symptoms, and solutions for common software configuration issues is crucial for effectively troubleshooting and resolving problems to ensure the reliability and performance of computer systems. One of the most common software configuration issues is compatibility problems, where software applications are not compatible with the underlying operating system, hardware, or other software components, resulting in crashes, errors, or performance issues. Compatibility problems can arise due to outdated software versions, incompatible drivers, conflicting dependencies, or changes in system configurations. To resolve compatibility problems, users can try updating software applications and drivers to the latest versions, checking for compatibility issues with hardware and other software components, or running software in compatibility mode or virtualized environments. Another common software configuration issue is misconfigured system settings, where software applications are not configured correctly to work with specific hardware devices, network environments, or user preferences, resulting in errors, crashes, or performance degradation. Misconfigured system settings can occur due to incorrect installation options, default configurations, or user preferences that conflict with application requirements. To resolve misconfigured system settings, users can try resetting application settings to default values, adjusting system settings to match application requirements, or reinstalling software with the correct configuration options. Another common software configuration issue is insufficient system resources, where software applications require more memory, CPU, disk space, or network bandwidth than available on the system, resulting in slow performance, crashes, or errors. Insufficient system resources can occur due to heavy system workload, memory leaks, or resource-intensive applications running concurrently. To resolve insufficient system resources, users can try closing unnecessary applications and background processes, upgrading hardware components, optimizing system configurations, or using resource monitoring tools to identify and address resource bottlenecks. Another common software configuration issue is permission problems, where software applications are not granted sufficient permissions to access required files, directories, or system resources, resulting in access denied errors, permission denied errors, or application crashes. Permission problems can occur due to restrictive security policies, incorrect file permissions, or user account settings that restrict application access. To resolve permission problems, users can try running applications with elevated privileges, adjusting file permissions to grant appropriate access rights, or modifying user account settings to allow application access. Another common software configuration issue is network connectivity problems, where software applications are unable to connect to remote servers, websites, or network resources due to network configuration issues, firewall restrictions, or DNS resolution errors. Network connectivity problems can occur due to misconfigured network settings, network hardware failures, or network infrastructure issues. To resolve network connectivity problems, users can try checking network settings, restarting network devices, disabling firewalls or security software temporarily, or using alternative network connections or protocols. Another common software configuration issue is outdated software, where software applications are not updated to the latest versions, patches, or security updates, resulting in compatibility issues, security vulnerabilities, or performance problems. Outdated software can occur due to neglecting software updates, disabling automatic updates, or using legacy software versions that are no longer supported by the vendor. To resolve outdated software issues, users can try installing software updates, patches, or security fixes released by the vendor, enabling automatic updates for critical software applications, or migrating to newer software versions that offer improved features and compatibility. Another common software configuration issue is software conflicts, where multiple software applications installed on the system interfere with each other's operation, resulting in crashes, errors, or unexpected behavior. Software conflicts can occur due to incompatible software versions, conflicting dependencies, or overlapping functionality between applications. To resolve software conflicts, users can try uninstalling conflicting applications, disabling unnecessary background processes and services, or using compatibility settings to isolate problematic applications. In summary, troubleshooting software configuration issues is an essential skill for IT professionals, system administrators, and users, as it allows them to identify and resolve problems that may arise due to misconfigured software settings, preferences, or options. By understanding the causes, symptoms, and solutions for common software configuration issues, users can effectively troubleshoot and resolve problems to ensure the reliability and performance of computer systems. Regular maintenance, updates, and backups are essential for preventing and mitigating software configuration issues and minimizing downtime and disruption caused by system failures.

Cybersecurity is a critical aspect of modern computing systems, encompassing strategies, technologies, and practices designed to protect computer systems, networks, and data from unauthorized access, cyber attacks, and data breaches. Understanding the basics of cybersecurity is essential for individuals, businesses, and organizations to safeguard their digital assets and mitigate cybersecurity risks effectively. One of the fundamental concepts of cybersecurity is confidentiality, which ensures that sensitive information is protected from unauthorized access, disclosure, or modification. Confidentiality is achieved through encryption, access controls, and data classification, which restrict access to sensitive data to authorized users and prevent unauthorized users from intercepting or tampering with data during transmission or storage. Another key concept of cybersecurity is integrity, which ensures that data remains accurate, complete, and unaltered throughout its lifecycle. Integrity is maintained through data validation, checksums, and digital signatures, which detect and prevent unauthorized modifications or tampering with data and ensure its authenticity and trustworthiness. Availability is another fundamental aspect of cybersecurity, ensuring that computer systems, networks, and data are accessible and usable by authorized users when needed. Availability is achieved through redundancy, fault tolerance, and disaster recovery planning, which ensure that systems can withstand hardware failures, software bugs, or cyber attacks and continue to operate effectively without interruption. Authentication is a core component of cybersecurity, verifying the identity of users, devices, or applications attempting to access computer systems, networks, or data. Authentication is achieved through passwords, biometrics, multi-factor authentication (MFA), and digital certificates, which authenticate users based on something they know, have, or are, and ensure that only authorized users can access sensitive resources. Authorization is closely related to authentication, determining the permissions and privileges granted to authenticated users, devices, or applications based on their roles, responsibilities, or security clearance levels. Authorization is achieved through access controls, role-based access control (RBAC), and least privilege principle, which restrict access to sensitive resources to authorized users and prevent unauthorized users from performing privileged actions. Risk management is a fundamental principle of cybersecurity, identifying, assessing, and mitigating cybersecurity risks to protect digital assets and achieve business objectives effectively. Risk management involves conducting risk assessments, implementing controls, and monitoring risks continuously to ensure that cybersecurity risks are managed proactively and aligned with organizational goals and priorities. Vulnerability management is another essential aspect of cybersecurity, identifying, prioritizing, and remedying security vulnerabilities in computer systems, networks, and applications to prevent cyber attacks and data breaches. Vulnerability management involves scanning systems for vulnerabilities, patching or mitigating vulnerabilities promptly, and implementing security best practices to minimize the risk of exploitation by cyber attackers. Incident response is a critical component of cybersecurity, preparing for, detecting, and responding to cybersecurity incidents promptly to minimize their impact and recover from them effectively. Incident response involves developing incident response plans, establishing incident response teams, and conducting incident simulations and drills to ensure that organizations can respond to cybersecurity incidents quickly, effectively, and efficiently. Security awareness and training are essential elements of cybersecurity, educating users, employees, and stakeholders about cybersecurity risks, best practices, and policies to promote a culture of security and accountability within organizations. Security awareness and training programs provide users with the knowledge, skills, and resources they need to recognize, prevent, and respond to cybersecurity threats effectively and help organizations build a strong security posture. Compliance and regulations are important considerations in cybersecurity, ensuring that organizations comply with applicable laws, regulations, and industry standards governing cybersecurity and data protection. Compliance and regulations may require organizations to implement specific security controls, privacy measures, and incident reporting procedures to protect sensitive data and mitigate cybersecurity risks effectively. In summary, the basics of cybersecurity encompass a wide range of concepts, principles, and practices designed to protect computer systems, networks, and data from cyber threats and vulnerabilities. By understanding the fundamentals of cybersecurity, individuals, businesses, and organizations can implement effective cybersecurity strategies, technologies, and controls to safeguard their digital assets and mitigate cybersecurity risks effectively. Continual learning, adaptation, and improvement are essential for maintaining a strong security posture and staying ahead of emerging cyber threats and challenges in today's rapidly evolving digital landscape. Identifying common security threats is essential for individuals, businesses, and organizations to protect their digital assets and sensitive information from malicious actors and cyber attacks. Cyber threats come in various forms and can target computer systems, networks, applications, and data, posing significant risks to confidentiality, integrity, and availability. One of the most common security threats is malware, malicious software designed to infiltrate, damage, or disrupt computer systems, steal sensitive information, or gain unauthorized access to networks and resources. Malware includes viruses, worms, Trojans, ransomware, spyware, and adware, which can infect systems through email attachments, malicious websites, infected files, or removable media and exploit vulnerabilities to compromise system security. To identify malware threats, users can use antivirus software, firewalls, and *intrusion detection systems to scan for and detect malicious activity, quarantine infected files, and prevent malware from spreading or executing on the system. Another common security threat is phishing, a social engineering attack where cyber criminals impersonate trusted entities, such as banks, government agencies, or reputable organizations, to trick users into revealing sensitive information, such as usernames, passwords, or financial data. Phishing attacks typically involve fraudulent emails, text messages, or phone calls that lure victims into clicking on malicious links, downloading infected attachments, or providing personal information, which can be used for identity theft, fraud, or unauthorized access to accounts. To identify phishing threats, users can look for signs of phishing, such as suspicious sender addresses, spelling and grammar errors, urgent requests for personal information, or unsolicited requests for financial transactions, and avoid clicking on links or providing sensitive information unless they can verify the authenticity of the sender. Another common security threat is ransomware, a type of malware that encrypts files or locks computer systems and demands a ransom payment from victims in exchange for decrypting files or restoring access to their systems. Ransomware attacks can occur through email attachments, malicious websites, or vulnerable software and can have devastating consequences, including data loss, financial losses, and business disruption. To identify ransomware threats, users can look for signs of ransomware infection, such as encrypted files with unusual file extensions, ransom notes on the desktop or* in affected folders, or unusual network activity indicating communication with command and control servers. Another common security threat is insider threats, where employees, contractors, or trusted individuals intentionally or unintentionally misuse their privileges to compromise system security, steal sensitive information, or sabotage operations. Insider threats can result from employee negligence, disgruntled employees, or malicious insiders seeking to profit from unauthorized access or leak confidential information. To identify insider threats, organizations can implement access controls, monitoring tools, and user behavior analytics to detect suspicious activities, unauthorized access attempts, or abnormal behavior patterns that may indicate insider threats and take appropriate action to mitigate risks and protect sensitive information. Another common security threat is distributed denial of service (DDoS) attacks, where attackers flood targeted computer systems, networks, or services with a large volume of traffic or requests to overwhelm their resources and disrupt their operations. DDoS attacks can result in service outages, downtime, or performance degradation, impacting the availability and reliability of critical services and systems. To identify DDoS threats, organizations can use DDoS mitigation services, intrusion detection systems, and traffic analysis tools to monitor network traffic, detect abnormal patterns, and mitigate DDoS attacks by filtering or blocking malicious traffic before it reaches the target. Another common security threat is zero-day exploits, where attackers exploit previously unknown vulnerabilities in software or *hardware to compromise systems, bypass security controls, or gain unauthorized access to sensitive information. Zero-day exploits can pose significant risks to organizations, as they leave systems vulnerable to cyber attacks until security patches or updates are released by vendors. To identify zero-day exploits, organizations can use vulnerability scanning tools, penetration testing, and threat intelligence feeds to identify and prioritize vulnerabilities based on their severity, exploitability, and potential impact on system security. In summary, identifying common security threats is essential for individuals, businesses, and organizations to protect their digital assets and sensitive information from cyber attacks and security breaches. By understanding the nature, characteristics, and tactics of common security threats, users can implement effective security measures, best practices, and controls to mitigate risks, safeguard their systems and networks, and maintain a strong security posture in today's constantly evolving threat landscape. Continual monitoring, detection, and response are essential for staying ahead of emerging threats and ensuring the resilience and security of digital assets and operations.*

The importance of data backup cannot be overstated in today's digital age, where businesses, organizations, and individuals rely heavily on digital data for their day-to-day operations, decision-making, and communication. Data backup is the process of creating copies of important files, documents, databases, and other digital assets and storing them in secondary or offsite locations to protect against data loss, corruption, or theft. Data loss can occur due to various reasons, including hardware failures, software bugs, human errors, cyber attacks, natural disasters, or accidental deletion, and can have devastating consequences for businesses and individuals alike. Without proper data backup measures in place, organizations risk losing critical business data, financial records, customer information, intellectual property, and other valuable assets, leading to financial losses, legal liabilities, reputational damage, and operational disruptions. For businesses, data backup is essential for ensuring business continuity, compliance with regulatory requirements, and protection of sensitive information against unauthorized access or disclosure. By regularly backing up data, organizations can minimize the impact of data loss incidents, recover lost or corrupted data quickly, and resume normal operations with minimal downtime, reducing the risk of revenue loss, customer dissatisfaction, or legal penalties. Data backup also plays a crucial role in disaster recovery planning, enabling organizations to restore data and systems to a previous state in the event of hardware failures, software glitches, or cyber attacks, and resume operations promptly without significant data loss or disruption. For individuals, data backup is equally important for protecting personal files, photos, videos, documents, and other digital assets against accidental deletion, device failures, or theft. Personal data, such as family photos, financial records, or important documents, holds sentimental and practical value and may be irreplaceable if lost or corrupted. By regularly backing up personal data to external hard drives, cloud storage services, or other backup solutions, individuals can safeguard their digital memories, preserve important documents, and ensure peace of mind knowing that their data is protected against unforeseen events. Data backup also provides an additional layer of security against cyber threats, such as ransomware, viruses, or malware, which can encrypt or delete data on infected systems and demand ransom payments from victims to restore access to their files. By maintaining up-to-date backups of critical data, organizations and individuals can mitigate the impact of ransomware attacks, restore affected systems from backup copies, and avoid paying ransom to cyber criminals, thereby minimizing financial losses and preserving data integrity. In addition to protecting against data loss, data backup is essential for data archival, long-term storage, and compliance with legal and regulatory requirements, such as data retention policies, privacy laws, or industry standards. By archiving historical data and maintaining backup copies for extended periods, organizations can meet legal and regulatory obligations, support auditing and compliance efforts, and preserve data for future analysis, research, or reference purposes. Furthermore, data backup promotes good data management practices, encourages data hygiene, and fosters a culture of data stewardship within organizations, where employees are encouraged to take responsibility for protecting and preserving valuable data assets. By educating employees about the importance of data backup, providing training on backup procedures, and implementing automated backup solutions, organizations can minimize the risk of data loss incidents, improve data resilience, and enhance overall cybersecurity posture. In summary, the importance of data backup cannot be overstated in today's digital world, where businesses, organizations, and individuals rely heavily on digital data for their operations, decision-making, and communication. Data backup is essential for protecting against data loss, ensuring business continuity, supporting disaster recovery efforts, and complying with legal and regulatory requirements. By implementing robust data backup strategies, organizations and individuals can safeguard their digital assets, mitigate the impact of data loss incidents, and preserve data integrity and availability in the face of evolving cyber threats and challenges.

Data recovery techniques are essential tools in the arsenal of IT professionals, system administrators, and *individuals alike, allowing them to retrieve lost, corrupted, or inaccessible data from storage devices such as hard drives, solid-state drives (SSDs), memory cards, USB drives, and RAID arrays. Data loss can occur due to various reasons, including accidental deletion, hardware failures, software errors, formatting errors, file system corruption, virus infections, or physical damage to storage media. Regardless of the cause, data recovery techniques can help restore lost data and minimize the impact of data loss incidents on businesses, organizations, and individuals. One of the most common data recovery techniques is file system repair, where damaged or corrupted file systems are repaired to restore access to files and folders stored on storage devices. File system repair tools scan storage media for errors, inconsistencies, or corruption in the file system structure, such as lost clusters, cross-linked files, or corrupted metadata, and attempt to repair or rebuild the file system to recover lost data. File system repair techniques vary depending on the file system type, such as NTFS, FAT32, exFAT, HFS+, or Ext4, and may involve running built-in file system repair utilities, such as CHKDSK on Windows or fsck on Linux, or using third-party disk repair tools to diagnose and fix file system errors. Another data recovery technique is data carving, where lost or deleted files are reconstructed and extracted from storage media based on their file signatures, headers, or footers, without relying on file system information. Data carving tools scan storage devices for raw data fragments or patterns that match known file formats, such as documents, images, videos,* or archives, and extract and reconstruct files based on file signatures and content analysis. Data carving techniques are particularly effective for recovering deleted files, overwritten files, or files from damaged file systems where file system metadata is missing or corrupted, but may result in incomplete or fragmented file recovery and require manual verification and validation of recovered files. Another data recovery technique is disk imaging, where bit-by-bit copies of storage devices are created and stored as disk images or disk clones to preserve the original data and facilitate data recovery operations. Disk imaging tools create exact replicas of storage devices, including partition tables, file systems, and data sectors, and store them as image files on separate storage media, such as external hard drives, network shares, or cloud storage services. Disk images can be used to perform data recovery operations, such as file system repair, data carving, or forensic analysis, without risking further damage to the original storage media, and serve as backups for disaster recovery purposes. Another data recovery technique is RAID data recovery, where data is recovered from redundant array of independent disks (RAID) arrays that have experienced failures, such as disk failures, controller failures, or RAID configuration errors. RAID data recovery techniques involve rebuilding RAID arrays, reconstructing data from redundant disks, and repairing or replacing failed disks to restore data redundancy and integrity. RAID data recovery tools and services vary depending on the RAID level, such as RAID 0, RAID 1, RAID 5, RAID 6, or RAID 10, and may require *specialized knowledge and expertise to diagnose and resolve RAID-related issues effectively. Another data recovery technique is data replication, where copies of data are synchronized and replicated across multiple storage devices, locations, or cloud servers to ensure data availability, fault tolerance, and disaster recovery. Data replication techniques involve creating mirror copies of data in real-time or near-real-time and replicating changes asynchronously or synchronously to secondary storage systems, such as backup servers, disaster recovery sites, or cloud storage platforms. Data replication solutions provide high availability and data redundancy, allowing organizations to recover quickly from data loss incidents, minimize downtime, and maintain business continuity in the event of hardware failures, natural disasters, or cyber attacks. In summary, data recovery techniques are essential tools for retrieving lost, corrupted, or inaccessible data from storage devices and minimizing the impact of data loss incidents on businesses, organizations, and individuals. By understanding and implementing data recovery techniques, IT professionals, system administrators, and individuals can recover valuable data, restore system functionality, and maintain data integrity and availability in the face of evolving threats and challenges in today's digital landscape. Continual learning, adaptation, and improvement are essential for staying abreast of new data recovery technologies, tools, and best practices and ensuring effective data recovery operations in response to data loss incidents.*

Remote access tools and technologies play a vital role in today's interconnected world, enabling users to access and control computers, networks, and data from remote locations, regardless of geographical boundaries or physical proximity. Remote access tools facilitate collaboration, support, troubleshooting, and remote administration for individuals, businesses, and organizations, allowing them to work more efficiently, improve productivity, and reduce costs associated with travel and on-site support. One of the most common remote access technologies is virtual private networks (VPNs), which establish secure, encrypted connections between remote users and corporate networks over the internet, allowing users to access network resources, such as files, applications, and printers, securely from anywhere in the world. VPNs use tunneling protocols, such as Point-to-Point Tunneling Protocol (PPTP), Layer 2 Tunneling Protocol (L2TP), Secure Socket Tunneling Protocol (SSTP), or Internet Protocol Security (IPsec), to encapsulate and encrypt data transmitted between remote clients and VPN servers, ensuring confidentiality, integrity, and privacy of communications over untrusted networks. Another common remote access technology is remote desktop software, which allows users to access and control remote computers or virtual desktops from their local devices, such as desktop computers, laptops, or mobile devices, using graphical user interfaces (GUIs) or command-line interfaces (CLIs). Remote desktop software provides remote users with a graphical desktop environment, keyboard, mouse, and display capabilities, allowing them to interact with remote computers as if they were physically present at the remote location, which is particularly useful for telecommuting, telework, or remote technical support scenarios. Popular remote desktop software solutions include Microsoft Remote Desktop, TeamViewer, AnyDesk, Splashtop, and VNC (Virtual Network Computing), which offer features such as screen sharing, file transfer, remote printing, and session recording to facilitate remote collaboration and support. Another remote access technology is remote administration tools (RATs), which enable IT administrators, system administrators, or helpdesk technicians to remotely manage and administer computer systems, servers, or network devices from a central location, using command-line interfaces (CLIs), scripting languages, or graphical user interfaces (GUIs). RATs provide administrators with remote access to system configuration settings, event logs, performance metrics, and troubleshooting tools, allowing them to diagnose and resolve technical issues, install software updates, configure security settings, and perform routine maintenance tasks without requiring physical access to remote systems, which improves operational efficiency and reduces downtime. Remote administration tools vary in complexity and functionality, ranging from built-in remote management features in operating systems, such as Windows Remote Management (WinRM) or

Secure Shell (SSH), to third-party remote administration software, such as PowerShell Remoting, Remote Desktop Services (RDS), or third-party remote management platforms like SolarWinds Remote Monitoring and Management (RMM) or ManageEngine Desktop Central. Another remote access technology is cloud-based remote access solutions, which provide users with on-demand access to remote desktops, applications, or virtual machines hosted in cloud environments, such as public clouds, private clouds, or hybrid clouds. Cloud-based remote access solutions eliminate the need for users to maintain and manage physical hardware or infrastructure, as cloud service providers handle the provisioning, scaling, and management of remote resources, allowing users to access and use computing resources on a pay-as-you-go basis, which reduces upfront costs and overhead associated with traditional IT infrastructure. Cloud-based remote access solutions offer flexibility, scalability, and agility, enabling organizations to quickly deploy and scale remote access capabilities to meet changing business requirements, support remote workforces, or facilitate disaster recovery and business continuity planning. Another remote access technology is remote monitoring and management (RMM) platforms, which provide IT service providers, managed service providers (MSPs), or enterprise IT teams with centralized monitoring, automation, and remote control capabilities for managing and supporting distributed IT infrastructures, such as networks, servers, endpoints, and devices. RMM platforms combine remote access, monitoring, patch management, antivirus management, backup and recovery, and automation features into integrated solutions, allowing IT administrators to monitor system health, detect and remediate issues proactively, enforce security policies, and deliver remote support services efficiently from a single console or dashboard. RMM platforms offer visibility, control, and automation across heterogeneous IT environments, enabling organizations to streamline IT operations, improve service levels, and reduce costs associated with manual intervention and on-site support visits. In summary, remote access tools and technologies play a crucial role in enabling remote work, supporting remote collaboration, and facilitating remote administration for individuals, businesses, and organizations in today's digital world. By leveraging remote access solutions, users can access and control computers, networks, and data from anywhere, at any time, enabling them to work more efficiently, improve productivity, and adapt to changing work environments and business needs. Continual innovation, security enhancements, and usability improvements are essential for advancing remote access technologies and addressing emerging challenges and opportunities in remote work and digital collaboration.

Troubleshooting over remote connections has become increasingly essential in today's digital landscape, where remote work and distributed teams are more prevalent than ever. As businesses and organizations rely heavily on technology for their operations, the ability to diagnose and resolve issues remotely has become a critical skill for IT professionals, system administrators, and technical support teams. Troubleshooting over remote connections involves identifying and resolving technical problems, errors, or issues with computer systems, networks, software applications, or devices without physically accessing the affected systems or locations. This often requires the use of remote access tools, communication platforms, and collaboration techniques to interact with remote users, diagnose problems, and implement solutions effectively. One of the key challenges of troubleshooting over remote connections is the limited visibility and access to remote systems, which can make it more challenging to diagnose and troubleshoot technical issues compared to on-site troubleshooting. Without physical access to the affected systems, IT professionals must rely on remote access tools, monitoring software, and diagnostic utilities to gather information about the system's configuration, performance, and behavior remotely. Remote access tools such as remote desktop software, SSH (Secure Shell), or VPN (Virtual Private Network) connections allow IT professionals to access remote systems remotely, view desktops, run commands, and perform troubleshooting tasks as if they were physically present at the remote location. However, remote troubleshooting may be hindered by network connectivity issues, firewall restrictions, or security policies that limit remote access to systems, requiring IT professionals to work closely with network administrators or security teams to ensure that remote access is allowed and secure. Another challenge of *troubleshooting over remote connections is the need to communicate effectively with remote users or customers to understand their technical issues, provide guidance, and gather relevant information to diagnose and resolve problems remotely. Effective communication skills, active listening, and empathy are essential for building rapport with remote users, gaining their trust, and eliciting accurate information about their technical issues, symptoms, and troubleshooting steps taken so far. Technical support teams may use remote communication platforms such as email, instant messaging, video conferencing, or phone calls to communicate with remote users, troubleshoot issues in real-time, and provide remote assistance and guidance throughout the troubleshooting process. Clear and concise communication is critical for ensuring that remote users understand the troubleshooting steps, follow instructions correctly, and provide relevant feedback to help diagnose and resolve technical issues efficiently. Another challenge of troubleshooting over remote connections is the lack of physical access to hardware components or peripherals, which can make it more challenging to diagnose and troubleshoot hardware-related issues remotely. Hardware troubleshooting may require remote users to perform physical checks, inspections, or tests on hardware components, such as power cables, connectors, or peripherals, under the guidance of IT professionals to identify potential hardware failures or malfunctions. Remote troubleshooting tools such as remote control software, diagnostic utilities, or hardware monitoring tools may be used to gather information about hardware status, temperature, or performance remotely and diagnose hardware-related issues without physical access to the hardware. However, hardware troubleshooting over remote connections may be limited by the availability of remote monitoring capabilities, hardware compatibility, or the complexity of hardware configurations, requiring IT professionals to collaborate closely with remote users and hardware vendors to diagnose and resolve hardware problems effectively. Another challenge of troubleshooting over remote connections is the need to troubleshoot complex technical issues that require specialized knowledge, expertise, or diagnostic tools that may not be available remotely. In such cases, IT professionals may need to escalate the issue to higher-level support teams, technical specialists, or vendors with the necessary skills, resources, or access to diagnose and resolve the problem effectively. Remote troubleshooting may involve collaborating with multiple stakeholders, teams, or vendors to coordinate troubleshooting efforts, share information, and implement solutions collectively, which requires effective communication, collaboration, and problem-solving skills to ensure that technical issues are resolved promptly and efficiently. In summary, troubleshooting over remote connections presents unique challenges and opportunities for IT professionals, system administrators, and technical support teams to diagnose and resolve technical issues remotely. By leveraging remote access tools, communication platforms, and collaboration techniques effectively, IT professionals can overcome the challenges of remote troubleshooting, provide timely and effective support to remote users, and maintain the reliability and performance of computer systems, networks, and devices in today's digital world. Continual learning, adaptation, and innovation are essential for developing and refining remote troubleshooting skills and techniques to address emerging challenges and opportunities in remote work and digital collaboration.*

Hands-on troubleshooting exercises are invaluable tools for IT professionals, system administrators, and aspiring technicians to develop and hone their troubleshooting skills, gain practical experience, and build confidence in diagnosing and resolving technical issues effectively. These exercises simulate real-world scenarios and challenges encountered in IT environments, allowing participants to apply their knowledge, problem-solving abilities, and technical expertise to identify root causes, implement solutions, and troubleshoot common and complex issues across different hardware, software, and network configurations. One of the key benefits of hands-on troubleshooting exercises is that they provide a safe and controlled environment for learners to experiment, make mistakes, and learn from their experiences without risking damage to production systems or data loss. Participants can explore various troubleshooting techniques, methodologies, and tools, such as diagnostic utilities, command-line interfaces, system logs, and remote access tools, to diagnose and resolve technical issues systematically and efficiently. Hands-on troubleshooting exercises often involve setting up lab environments or virtualized environments using virtual machines, emulators, or cloud-based platforms, where participants can practice troubleshooting scenarios in isolation or as part of a team, collaborate with peers, and share insights and best practices for solving technical problems. These exercises may cover a wide range of topics and skills, including hardware troubleshooting, software debugging, network troubleshooting, security incident response, data recovery, and performance tuning, to address the diverse challenges faced by IT professionals in their daily work. For example, hardware troubleshooting exercises may involve diagnosing and resolving common hardware failures or malfunctions, such as disk drive failures, memory errors, CPU overheating, or power supply issues, using diagnostic tools, hardware diagnostics, and physical inspection techniques to identify faulty components and replace them as needed. Software troubleshooting exercises may focus on diagnosing and resolving software errors, bugs, or compatibility issues in operating systems, applications, or drivers, using troubleshooting methodologies such as divide-and-conquer, binary search, or rollback-and-isolate to isolate and fix problems systematically without disrupting system stability or user productivity. Network troubleshooting exercises may involve diagnosing and resolving connectivity issues, performance problems, or security vulnerabilities in computer networks, using network monitoring tools, packet sniffers, protocol analyzers, and network diagnostic utilities to analyze network traffic, identify bottlenecks, and troubleshoot network configuration issues, such as IP address conflicts, DNS resolution errors, or firewall misconfigurations. Security incident response exercises may simulate cyber attacks, malware infections, or data breaches, where participants are tasked with detecting, analyzing, and mitigating security incidents, using security monitoring tools, intrusion detection systems, malware analysis tools, and incident response playbooks to contain the threat, investigate the root cause, and restore affected systems and data to a secure state. Data recovery exercises may involve recovering lost or corrupted data from storage devices, such as hard drives, solid-state drives (SSDs), memory cards, or USB drives, using data recovery software, forensic tools, or hardware repair techniques to retrieve deleted files, repair corrupted file systems, or extract data from damaged storage media safely and effectively. Performance tuning exercises may focus on optimizing system performance, resource utilization, or response times in computer systems, servers, or applications, using performance monitoring tools, profiling tools, benchmarking tools, and performance tuning techniques to identify performance bottlenecks, optimize system configurations, and improve overall system efficiency and responsiveness. In summary, hands-on troubleshooting exercises are invaluable learning experiences for IT professionals, system administrators, and aspiring technicians to develop and refine their troubleshooting skills, gain practical experience, and build confidence in diagnosing and resolving technical issues effectively. By participating in hands-on troubleshooting exercises, learners can explore different troubleshooting techniques, methodologies, and tools, practice problem-solving in real-world scenarios, and collaborate with peers to *share insights and best practices for solving technical problems. Continual practice, experimentation, and reflection are essential for mastering troubleshooting skills and staying abreast of emerging technologies, trends, and challenges in the dynamic field of information technology.*

Developing problem-solving strategies is essential for individuals, teams, and organizations to effectively address challenges, overcome obstacles, and achieve their goals in various aspects of life, work, and problem-solving endeavors. Problem-solving is a cognitive process that involves identifying, analyzing, and solving problems or obstacles encountered in achieving desired outcomes, objectives, or results. Developing problem-solving strategies requires a combination of critical thinking, creativity, collaboration, and perseverance to tackle complex issues, make informed decisions, and implement effective solutions systematically. One of the key steps in developing problem-solving strategies is defining the problem clearly and precisely, which involves identifying the root cause, scope, and impact of the problem, clarifying the desired outcome or goal, and understanding the constraints, limitations, and stakeholders involved in addressing the problem. Defining the problem helps focus efforts, prioritize tasks, and set clear objectives for problem-solving activities, enabling individuals or teams to develop targeted strategies and action plans to achieve desired results. Another important step in developing problem-solving strategies is analyzing the problem thoroughly, which involves gathering relevant information, data, and evidence about the problem, exploring different perspectives, and identifying underlying causes, patterns, or trends that contribute to the problem. Analyzing the problem helps uncover hidden assumptions, biases, or constraints that may affect problem-solving efforts, enabling individuals or teams to make informed decisions, generate insights, and develop effective solutions that address the root causes of the problem effectively. Once the problem has been defined and analyzed, the next step in developing problem-solving strategies is generating potential solutions or alternatives, which involves brainstorming ideas, evaluating options, and considering different approaches or perspectives to solving the problem creatively. Generating solutions requires openness to new ideas, willingness to take risks, and willingness to challenge assumptions or conventional thinking, enabling individuals or teams to explore innovative or unconventional solutions that may lead to breakthroughs or improvements in problem-solving outcomes. After generating potential solutions, the next step in developing problem-solving strategies is evaluating and selecting the best solution or course of action, which involves weighing the pros and cons of each option, assessing feasibility, impact, and risks, and considering factors such as cost, time, resources, and stakeholders' needs or preferences. Evaluating solutions requires critical thinking, logical reasoning, and decision-making skills to determine the most effective and practical solution that aligns with the desired outcome or goal, enabling individuals or teams to move forward with confidence and conviction in implementing the chosen solution. Once a solution has been selected, the final step in developing problem-solving strategies is implementing and monitoring the solution effectively, which involves planning and organizing tasks, allocating resources, and executing the action plan to implement the solution systematically. Implementing the solution requires clear communication, coordination, and collaboration among stakeholders, as well as flexibility and adaptability to address unforeseen challenges or obstacles that may arise during implementation. Monitoring the solution involves tracking progress, collecting feedback, and evaluating outcomes to ensure that the solution achieves the desired results and meets stakeholders' expectations, enabling individuals or teams to make adjustments, improvements, or refinements as needed to optimize problem-solving outcomes and achieve sustainable results. In summary, developing problem-solving strategies is a dynamic and iterative process that requires creativity, critical thinking, collaboration, and perseverance to address challenges, overcome obstacles, and achieve desired outcomes effectively. By following a systematic approach to problem-solving, individuals, teams, and organizations can develop effective strategies, make informed decisions, and implement practical solutions that lead to positive results and continuous improvement in various aspects of life, work, and problem-solving endeavors. Continual learning, reflection, and adaptation are essential for refining problem-solving skills and staying abreast of emerging challenges and opportunities in today's rapidly changing world.

BOOK 2
MASTERING COMMON IT ISSUES
INTERMEDIATE TROUBLESHOOTING TECHNIQUES

ROB BOTWRIGHT

Network protocol analysis is a fundamental aspect of network troubleshooting, security, and optimization, involving the examination and interpretation of network traffic to understand how communication protocols are used, identify abnormal behavior, and diagnose network-related issues. At its core, network protocol analysis aims to capture, inspect, and analyze the packets exchanged between devices on a network to gain insights into network activity, performance, and security posture. By scrutinizing the structure and content of network packets, analysts can detect anomalies, detect potential security threats, and optimize network performance. Network protocol analysis relies on specialized tools known as packet analyzers or network protocol analyzers, which capture and decode network packets in real-time or from packet capture files for analysis. These tools provide detailed visibility into network traffic, allowing analysts to examine packet headers, payloads, and metadata to identify communication patterns, detect errors, and troubleshoot connectivity issues. One of the primary goals of network protocol analysis is to understand how different protocols interact within a network environment, including the transmission control protocol (TCP), internet protocol (IP), user datagram protocol (UDP), and application-layer protocols such as hypertext transfer protocol (HTTP), domain name system (DNS), and simple mail transfer protocol (SMTP). By dissecting network packets and analyzing protocol headers, analysts can determine the source and destination of traffic, the types of services or applications being used, and the protocols involved in communication, enabling them to identify misconfigurations, bottlenecks, or security vulnerabilities that may impact network performance or integrity. Network protocol analysis is also crucial for troubleshooting network-related issues, such as connectivity problems, latency issues, or service disruptions, by providing insights into the root causes of problems and guiding remediation efforts. By examining packet captures and analyzing network traffic patterns, analysts can pinpoint the location and nature of network problems, such as packet loss, congestion, or misconfigured devices, and take appropriate actions to resolve them effectively. For example, if a network application is experiencing slow response times, analysts can use network protocol analysis to identify the source of latency, such as network congestion, packet retransmissions, or server-side delays, and implement optimizations to improve application performance. Furthermore, network protocol analysis plays a vital role in network security by enabling analysts to detect and mitigate security threats, such as malware infections, denial-of-service (DoS) attacks, or data exfiltration attempts, by monitoring network traffic for suspicious behavior and identifying indicators of compromise (IOCs). By analyzing packet payloads, inspecting network flows, and correlating events across different *network segments, analysts can identify anomalous patterns, detect known attack signatures, and respond to security incidents promptly, reducing the risk of data breaches or unauthorized access to sensitive information. Network protocol analysis is also essential for optimizing network performance and efficiency by identifying opportunities to streamline communication, reduce latency, and improve resource utilization. By analyzing network traffic patterns, identifying bandwidth-intensive applications or protocols, and optimizing network configurations, analysts can enhance network performance, scalability, and reliability, ensuring that critical applications and services operate smoothly and efficiently. Additionally, network protocol analysis can help organizations enforce network policies, such as quality of service (QoS) policies, access control lists (ACLs), or bandwidth management rules, by monitoring compliance with policy rules, detecting policy violations, and enforcing policy enforcement actions as needed. In summary, network protocol analysis is a critical process for understanding, troubleshooting, and securing computer networks, providing valuable insights into network activity, performance, and security posture. By leveraging specialized tools and techniques for capturing, inspecting, and analyzing network packets, analysts can gain deep visibility into network traffic, identify anomalies, diagnose problems, and mitigate security threats effectively. Continual learning, adaptation, and collaboration are essential for staying abreast of new protocols, technologies, and threats and ensuring that network protocol analysis remains an effective tool for maintaining the integrity, reliability, and security of modern networks.*

Troubleshooting network latency is a critical aspect of maintaining optimal performance and user experience in computer networks, as latency can significantly impact the responsiveness and efficiency of networked applications, services, and communication. Network latency refers to the delay or lag experienced when data packets travel between source and destination points on a network, often measured in milliseconds (ms), and is influenced by various factors, including network congestion, packet loss, bandwidth limitations, and distance between endpoints. Identifying and resolving network latency issues requires a systematic approach, involving the analysis of network traffic patterns, performance metrics, and configuration settings to pinpoint the root causes of latency and implement effective solutions. One of the first steps in troubleshooting network latency is to measure and monitor network performance using network monitoring tools, such as ping, traceroute, or network analyzers, to assess latency levels, identify latency hotspots, and track changes in latency over time. By collecting performance data and analyzing latency metrics, network administrators can gain insights into the behavior and characteristics of network traffic, enabling them to identify potential sources of latency and prioritize troubleshooting efforts accordingly. Another common cause of network latency is network congestion, which occurs when network bandwidth is insufficient to accommodate the volume of data traffic generated by networked devices, leading to queuing delays, packet drops, and increased latency. Troubleshooting network congestion involves identifying the congested network segments, analyzing traffic patterns, and implementing congestion management techniques, such as traffic shaping, prioritization, or load balancing, to alleviate congestion and improve network performance. Additionally, packet loss can contribute to network latency by requiring retransmissions of lost packets, resulting in increased round-trip times (RTTs) and degraded application performance. Troubleshooting packet loss involves identifying the causes of packet loss, such as network errors, buffer overflows, or faulty network devices, and implementing measures to reduce packet loss, such as optimizing network configurations, upgrading hardware, or improving network resilience and redundancy. Furthermore, network latency can be affected by the quality and reliability of network connections, particularly in wireless networks or wide area networks (WANs) with long distances between endpoints. Troubleshooting network connectivity issues involves testing network links, diagnosing signal interference or attenuation, and optimizing network configurations, such as adjusting transmission power levels, channel frequencies, or antenna placement, to improve signal strength and reliability and reduce latency. Moreover, network latency can be exacerbated by inefficient network protocols or communication patterns, such as excessive handshakes, retransmissions, or inefficient data transfer mechanisms, which can introduce unnecessary delays and overhead in network traffic. Troubleshooting protocol inefficiencies involves analyzing protocol behavior, optimizing protocol settings, or implementing protocol enhancements, such as using connection pooling, pipelining, or compression techniques, to reduce latency and improve protocol efficiency. Additionally, network latency can be influenced by hardware limitations, such as outdated network equipment, insufficient processing power, or inadequate memory resources, which can bottleneck network performance and introduce latency into network traffic. Troubleshooting hardware limitations involves upgrading outdated hardware, optimizing hardware configurations, or implementing hardware acceleration techniques, such as offloading packet processing tasks to dedicated network processors or specialized hardware components, to improve network performance and reduce latency. Furthermore, network latency can be impacted by environmental factors, such as temperature, humidity, or electromagnetic interference, which can affect the reliability and stability of network infrastructure components, such as routers, switches, or cables. Troubleshooting environmental factors involves monitoring environmental conditions, implementing environmental controls, such as air conditioning or shielding, and protecting network equipment from physical damage or exposure to environmental hazards to ensure optimal performance and reliability. In summary, troubleshooting network latency requires a systematic approach, involving the *identification, analysis, and resolution of various factors that contribute to latency in computer networks. By measuring and monitoring network performance, identifying latency hotspots, and implementing targeted solutions to address network congestion, packet loss, connectivity issues, protocol inefficiencies, hardware limitations, and environmental factors, network administrators can optimize network performance, improve user experience, and ensure the reliability and responsiveness of networked applications and services. Continual monitoring, analysis, and optimization are essential for maintaining optimal network performance and minimizing latency in today's interconnected and data-driven world.*

Advanced OS error diagnosis is a crucial skill for IT professionals, system administrators, and technical support teams to effectively troubleshoot and resolve complex issues encountered in operating systems. Operating systems serve as the foundation for computer systems, providing essential services and managing hardware resources, software applications, and user interactions, making it essential to diagnose and resolve errors promptly to ensure system stability, reliability, and performance. Advanced OS error diagnosis involves understanding the underlying causes of errors, analyzing system logs, and leveraging diagnostic tools and techniques to identify and resolve issues efficiently. One of the key aspects of advanced OS error diagnosis is understanding the different types of errors that can occur in operating systems, including kernel panics, system crashes, application errors, device driver failures, and system hangs. Kernel panics occur when the operating system's kernel encounters a fatal error or inconsistency that it cannot recover from, resulting in the system halting and displaying a diagnostic message or kernel panic screen. System crashes occur when critical system processes or components fail, causing the system to become unresponsive or unstable, often resulting in the infamous "blue screen of death" (BSOD) on Windows systems or kernel panic on Unix-like systems. Application errors occur when software applications encounter programming bugs, memory leaks, or resource conflicts that lead to unexpected behavior or crashes, requiring debugging and troubleshooting to identify and fix the underlying issues. Device driver failures occur when device drivers, which are software components that facilitate communication between hardware devices and the operating system, encounter compatibility issues, configuration errors, or hardware malfunctions, leading to device malfunctions or system instability. System hangs occur when the operating system becomes unresponsive or sluggish due to resource exhaustion, deadlock conditions, or software bugs, requiring intervention to restore normal operation and prevent data loss or system crashes. Another aspect of advanced OS error diagnosis is analyzing system logs and diagnostic information to understand the context and circumstances surrounding errors, such as timestamps, error codes, error messages, and system events recorded in log files, event logs, or crash dumps. System logs provide valuable insights into system activity, error conditions, and performance metrics, enabling administrators to identify patterns, trends, or correlations between events and errors, which can help diagnose root causes and prioritize troubleshooting efforts effectively. Analyzing system logs may involve using log analysis tools, scripting languages, or command-line utilities to parse, filter, and aggregate log data, allowing administrators to search for specific error messages, track changes over time, and correlate events across different log sources to identify underlying issues or patterns. Additionally, advanced OS error diagnosis involves leveraging diagnostic tools and utilities provided by the operating system or third-party vendors to diagnose and troubleshoot errors efficiently. Operating systems typically include built-in diagnostic tools and utilities, such as system information tools, performance monitoring tools, system recovery options, and troubleshooting wizards, that can help identify and resolve common issues, such as disk errors, memory problems, or startup failures. Third-party diagnostic tools and utilities offer additional capabilities and features for diagnosing and troubleshooting operating system errors, such as disk diagnostic tools, memory testing utilities, system optimization software, and remote troubleshooting solutions, which can complement built-in tools and provide advanced diagnostics and remediation options for complex issues. Moreover, advanced OS error diagnosis involves following best practices and methodologies for systematic troubleshooting, such as the divide-and-conquer approach, which involves isolating and testing individual components or subsystems to identify the root cause of a problem systematically. Other troubleshooting methodologies, such as root cause analysis (RCA), fault isolation, and error propagation analysis, can help identify the underlying causes of errors and their impact on system behavior, enabling administrators to implement targeted solutions and preventive measures to mitigate future occurrences. Furthermore, advanced OS error diagnosis requires effective communication, collaboration, and documentation to share diagnostic information, coordinate troubleshooting efforts, and track resolutions effectively. Collaborative troubleshooting involves leveraging knowledge bases, online forums, peer networks, and vendor support resources to access expertise, share insights, and exchange best practices for diagnosing and resolving operating system errors efficiently. Documenting troubleshooting steps, findings, and solutions in a knowledge base, incident report, or troubleshooting guide helps capture institutional knowledge, facilitate knowledge sharing, and improve the efficiency and effectiveness of future troubleshooting efforts. In summary, advanced OS error diagnosis is an essential skill for IT professionals, system administrators, and technical support teams to effectively diagnose and resolve complex issues encountered in operating systems. By understanding the different types of errors, analyzing system logs, leveraging diagnostic tools and techniques, following best practices and methodologies, and fostering communication and collaboration, administrators can diagnose and resolve operating system errors efficiently, ensure system stability and reliability, and minimize downtime and disruptions in computer systems and networks. Continual learning, experimentation, and adaptation are essential for developing and refining advanced OS error diagnosis skills and staying abreast of emerging technologies, trends, and challenges in the dynamic field of information technology. System recovery methods are essential procedures for restoring computer systems to a functional state after experiencing critical failures, errors, or malware infections, ensuring data integrity, system stability, and user productivity. System recovery encompasses a range of techniques, tools, and procedures designed to recover lost or corrupted data, repair damaged system files, and restore system settings to a known good state, minimizing downtime and disruptions in operations. One of the primary system recovery methods is using system restore points, which are snapshots of the system's configuration and settings taken at specific points in time, allowing users to revert the system to a previous state in case of problems. System restore points capture critical system files, registry settings, and application configurations, enabling users to roll back changes made to the system, such as software installations, driver updates, or system modifications, that may have caused instability or errors. By restoring the system to a previous restore point, users can undo harmful changes, resolve system errors, and recover from software-related issues without affecting personal files or data. Another common system recovery method is using backup and restore solutions, which involve creating copies of critical data, files, and system configurations and storing them in a secure location, such as an external hard drive, cloud storage service, or network-attached storage (NAS) device, for safekeeping and disaster recovery purposes. Backup solutions typically include features for scheduling automated backups, selecting specific files or folders to back up, and encrypting data for security, allowing users to protect against data loss, accidental deletion, or hardware failures by restoring backed-up data to its original state. By regularly backing up critical data and system configurations, users can ensure that they have a reliable backup copy to restore from in case of emergencies, such as hard drive failures, ransomware attacks, or natural disasters, minimizing the risk of data loss and downtime. Additionally, system recovery methods may involve using built-in recovery options provided by the operating system, such as Windows Recovery Environment (WinRE) on Windows systems or macOS Recovery on Mac systems, which offer tools and utilities for troubleshooting and repairing common system issues. Windows Recovery Environment provides a range of recovery options, such as startup repair, system restore, system image recovery, and command prompt access, allowing users to diagnose and fix problems that prevent Windows from booting properly, restore system files, or perform advanced troubleshooting tasks. Similarly, macOS Recovery provides utilities for repairing disk errors, reinstalling macOS, restoring from Time Machine backups, and accessing terminal commands, enabling users to troubleshoot and recover from system failures, disk corruption, or software problems on Mac computers. Moreover, system recovery methods may involve using third-party recovery tools and utilities, such as data recovery software, disk imaging tools, or system repair utilities, which offer advanced features and capabilities for recovering lost or deleted files, repairing disk errors, and troubleshooting system issues. Data recovery software can scan storage devices for lost or deleted files, partitions, or volumes and recover them to a safe location, allowing users to retrieve accidentally deleted files, recover files from formatted or corrupted disks, or restore data from damaged storage media. Disk imaging tools can create exact copies or snapshots of disk partitions or entire disks, allowing users to restore the entire system to a known good state, clone disks, or migrate to new hardware seamlessly. Additionally, system repair utilities can diagnose and fix common system errors, repair damaged system files, and optimize system performance, providing users with tools for maintaining system health and stability. In summary, system recovery methods are essential for restoring computer systems to a functional state after experiencing critical failures, errors, or malware infections, ensuring data integrity, system stability, and user productivity. By leveraging techniques such as system restore points, backup and restore solutions, built-in recovery options, and third-party recovery tools and utilities, users can recover lost or corrupted data, repair damaged system files, and restore system settings to a known good state, minimizing downtime and disruptions in operations. Continual backups, proactive maintenance, and disaster recovery planning are essential for mitigating the impact of system failures and ensuring business continuity in today's digital environment.

Hardware compatibility issues are common challenges faced by computer users, IT professionals, and system administrators when integrating new hardware components into existing computer systems or when upgrading system configurations. These issues arise when there is a mismatch between the hardware components, such as processors, motherboards, graphics cards, memory modules, storage devices, or peripherals, and the system architecture, operating system, device drivers, or firmware, resulting in system instability, functionality limitations, or hardware malfunctions. Understanding and addressing hardware compatibility issues is essential for ensuring the smooth operation, reliability, and performance of computer systems and minimizing the risk of data loss, system crashes, or hardware damage. One of the main causes of hardware compatibility issues is the lack of adherence to industry standards, specifications, or interoperability guidelines by hardware manufacturers, leading to inconsistencies in hardware implementations and compatibility conflicts with other components or systems. For example, incompatible memory modules may not be recognized by the motherboard or may operate at lower speeds than specified, leading to system crashes or performance degradation. Similarly, mismatched processor sockets or chipset architectures may prevent CPUs from being installed or functioning correctly in motherboards, resulting in compatibility issues and system instability. Another common cause of hardware compatibility issues is software dependencies, such as device drivers, firmware updates, or operating system requirements, that are not properly installed, configured, or updated to support new hardware components or features. Device drivers are essential software components that facilitate communication between hardware devices and the operating system, translating high-level commands and requests from the operating system into low-level instructions and signals that control hardware behavior. Incompatible or outdated device drivers may not fully support new hardware features or functionalities, leading to device malfunctions, performance issues, or system crashes. Similarly, firmware updates, which are software programs embedded in hardware devices to control device operation and behavior, may be incompatible with other hardware components or system configurations, resulting in firmware conflicts or compatibility issues that affect device functionality or performance. Additionally, hardware compatibility issues may arise due to differences in hardware architectures, such as processor instruction sets, memory addressing modes, or bus interfaces, which can affect the compatibility and interoperability of hardware components with each other or with the operating system. For example, a 64-bit processor may not be compatible with a 32-bit operating system, or a motherboard with a PCIe 3.0 slot may not be compatible with a PCIe 4.0 graphics card, resulting in compatibility conflicts or performance limitations. Furthermore, hardware compatibility issues may manifest as compatibility conflicts between hardware components and peripheral devices, such as printers, scanners, external storage devices, or input devices, which rely on standardized communication protocols, interfaces, or drivers to interact with computer systems. For example, a USB 3.0 device may not be recognized or function correctly when connected to a USB 2.0 port, or a graphics card may not support the display resolution or refresh rate of a monitor, resulting in compatibility issues or limited functionality. Moreover, hardware compatibility issues may be exacerbated by firmware bugs, hardware defects, or manufacturing tolerances that affect the reliability, performance, or compatibility of hardware components with other devices or systems. Firmware bugs or hardware defects may cause intermittent failures, system crashes, or data corruption, making it challenging to diagnose and resolve compatibility issues effectively. Manufacturing tolerances, such as variations in component specifications or quality control processes, may result in inconsistencies in hardware performance or behavior, leading to compatibility conflicts or interoperability issues that affect system stability or functionality. In summary, hardware compatibility issues are common challenges faced by computer users, IT professionals, and system administrators when integrating new hardware components into existing computer systems or when upgrading system configurations. By understanding the causes of hardware compatibility issues, such as inconsistencies in hardware implementations, software dependencies, hardware architectures, peripheral compatibility, firmware bugs, or manufacturing tolerances, users can take proactive measures to identify, diagnose, and resolve compatibility conflicts effectively, ensuring the smooth operation, reliability, and performance of computer systems. Continual monitoring, testing, and validation of hardware configurations and compatibility are essential for minimizing the risk of compatibility issues and ensuring the compatibility and interoperability of hardware components with other devices and systems in today's diverse and interconnected computing environments.

Application debugging methods are essential techniques employed by software developers, quality assurance engineers, and system administrators to identify, diagnose, and resolve software bugs, errors, or unexpected behaviors in computer applications, ensuring the reliability, stability, and performance of software systems. Debugging is a systematic process that involves analyzing the behavior of software applications, identifying the root causes of issues, and implementing corrective measures to fix problems and improve software quality. There are various debugging methods and tools available to developers for troubleshooting and resolving software issues, each with its strengths, limitations, and best practices. One of the primary debugging methods is using logging and output statements, which involve inserting diagnostic messages, status updates, or variable values into the code at strategic points to track the execution flow and state of the application during runtime. Logging and output statements provide visibility into the internal workings of the application, allowing developers to monitor variables, function calls, and program state, identify abnormal behaviors or error conditions, and trace the sequence of events leading to software bugs or failures. By strategically placing logging statements throughout the codebase and analyzing the output generated during program execution, developers can gain insights into the causes of issues, validate assumptions, and narrow down the scope of investigation to specific areas of code or functionality. Another common debugging method is using breakpoints and stepping through code, which involves pausing the execution of the program at specific breakpoints or lines of code and examining the program state, variable values, and call stack using a debugger tool or integrated development environment (IDE). Breakpoints allow developers to inspect the internal state of the application, evaluate expressions, and step through code line by line, enabling them to identify the precise location and context of software bugs, understand the flow of execution, and diagnose the root causes of issues effectively. By setting breakpoints strategically and stepping through code systematically, developers can isolate problematic code segments, observe how data changes over time, and test hypotheses to identify and fix software bugs efficiently. Additionally, code review and peer collaboration are effective debugging methods that involve soliciting feedback, insights, and suggestions from other developers, team members, or stakeholders to identify potential issues, validate assumptions, and improve the quality of code. Code reviews provide an opportunity for developers to review each other's code, identify logic errors, coding standards violations, or performance bottlenecks, and share best practices, alternative approaches, or debugging tips to address issues collaboratively. By leveraging the collective knowledge, experience, and perspectives of team members, developers can uncover blind spots, discover hidden bugs, and improve the overall quality, maintainability, and reliability of software applications. Moreover, using automated testing and debugging tools is a valuable method for detecting and diagnosing software bugs, errors, or vulnerabilities early in the development lifecycle, ensuring that software meets functional requirements, performance criteria, and quality standards. Automated testing tools, such as unit testing frameworks, integration testing suites, or code analysis tools, enable developers to execute predefined test cases, simulate user interactions, and verify the correctness of software behavior automatically, helping detect regression bugs, boundary conditions, or edge cases that may not be apparent during manual testing. Similarly, debugging tools, such as memory profilers, code analyzers, or runtime monitors, provide developers with insights into runtime performance, memory usage, or code coverage, enabling them to identify memory leaks, resource conflicts, or performance bottlenecks and optimize software for better reliability and efficiency. Furthermore, leveraging error handling and exception handling techniques is a proactive debugging method that involves anticipating potential errors, failures, or exceptional conditions and implementing mechanisms to handle them gracefully, prevent crashes, and maintain application stability. Error handling involves using try-catch blocks, exception objects, or error codes to detect and handle runtime errors, such as null pointer exceptions, division by zero errors, or file not *found exceptions, in a controlled manner, enabling applications to recover from errors, provide meaningful feedback to users, and continue executing without interruption. By implementing robust error handling mechanisms and logging error messages, developers can diagnose the causes of errors, capture diagnostic information, and guide users through troubleshooting steps to resolve issues effectively. In summary, application debugging methods are essential techniques employed by software developers, quality assurance engineers, and system administrators to identify, diagnose, and resolve software bugs, errors, or unexpected behaviors in computer applications. By leveraging debugging methods such as logging and output statements, breakpoints and stepping through code, code review and peer collaboration, automated testing and debugging tools, and error handling and exception handling techniques, developers can detect, diagnose, and fix software issues efficiently, ensuring the reliability, stability, and performance of software systems. Continual learning, experimentation, and adaptation are essential for mastering debugging skills and staying abreast of new tools, techniques, and best practices in the dynamic field of software development. Resolving application crashes is a critical task for computer users, IT professionals, and software developers alike, as crashes can disrupt productivity, lead to data loss, and undermine user confidence in software applications. An application crash occurs when a software program terminates unexpectedly due to a fatal error, unhandled exception, or system resource issue, resulting in the program abruptly closing without warning or displaying an error message to the user. Resolving application crashes involves identifying the root causes of crashes, diagnosing underlying issues, and implementing corrective measures to prevent future occurrences and restore application stability. One of the first steps in resolving application crashes is gathering diagnostic information about the crash, such as error messages, crash logs, system events, and user reports, to understand the circumstances and context surrounding the crash. Error messages and crash logs often contain valuable clues about the nature and severity of the crash, including error codes, memory addresses, stack traces, and timestamps, which can help pinpoint the root causes of crashes and guide troubleshooting efforts. Analyzing system events and user reports can provide additional insights into the frequency, patterns, and triggers of crashes, such as specific user actions, environmental conditions, or system configurations, which can help identify commonalities and trends among crash incidents. By collecting and analyzing diagnostic information systematically, IT professionals and software developers can gain a better understanding of the factors contributing to crashes and prioritize troubleshooting efforts effectively. Additionally, diagnosing application crashes involves reproducing the crash in a controlled environment, such as a development or testing environment, to isolate and replicate the conditions under which the crash occurs, enabling developers to observe the behavior of the application, capture relevant data, and troubleshoot the issue methodically. Reproducing crashes may involve following specific steps or sequences of actions reported by users, configuring system settings or environment variables, or simulating real-world scenarios to trigger the crash consistently. By reproducing crashes reliably, developers can validate reported issues, verify potential fixes, and evaluate the effectiveness of proposed solutions before deploying them to production environments. Moreover, analyzing the source code of the application is a crucial step in diagnosing and resolving application crashes, as crashes are often caused by programming errors, logic bugs, or memory corruption issues in the codebase. By reviewing the source code, developers can identify potential vulnerabilities, code paths, or error-handling mechanisms that may be contributing to crashes, such as null pointer dereferences, buffer overflows, or unhandled exceptions, and implement corrective measures to address them. Code analysis tools, static analysis tools, and debuggers can assist developers in identifying potential code defects, security vulnerabilities, or performance bottlenecks, enabling them to refactor code, fix bugs, or optimize algorithms to improve application stability and reliability. Additionally, debugging the application in a development environment using a debugger tool or integrated development environment (IDE) is an effective technique for diagnosing and resolving application crashes, as debuggers provide developers with real-time insights into the execution flow, variable values, and call stack of the application during runtime.*

By setting breakpoints, stepping through code, and inspecting variables, developers can trace the sequence of events leading to the crash, identify abnormal behaviors or unexpected conditions, and diagnose the root causes of crashes systematically. Debugging tools also offer features for analyzing memory usage, detecting memory leaks, or profiling performance, which can help developers identify memory-related issues or resource constraints that may be contributing to crashes. Furthermore, updating the application and its dependencies to the latest versions, patches, or hotfixes is a proactive measure for preventing and mitigating application crashes, as software updates often include bug fixes, security patches, and performance improvements that address known issues and vulnerabilities. By staying current with software updates and following best practices for software maintenance and deployment, IT professionals and software developers can minimize the risk of application crashes caused by outdated or incompatible software versions, deprecated dependencies, or unpatched security vulnerabilities. Additionally, implementing robust error handling and exception handling mechanisms in the application code can help mitigate the impact of unexpected errors, exceptions, or runtime failures on application stability and user experience. By anticipating potential failure scenarios, handling errors gracefully, and providing meaningful error messages or recovery options to users, developers can improve the resilience, reliability, and usability of the application, reducing the likelihood of crashes and enhancing user satisfaction. In summary, resolving application crashes requires a systematic approach that involves gathering diagnostic information, reproducing crashes, analyzing source code, debugging the application, updating software dependencies, and implementing robust error handling mechanisms. By identifying and addressing the root causes of crashes effectively, IT professionals and software developers can improve application stability, reliability, and user experience, ensuring that software applications perform as intended and meet the needs of users and stakeholders. Continual monitoring, testing, and refinement are essential for maintaining application stability and preventing future crashes in today's dynamic and evolving software landscape.

Performance monitoring tools are essential instruments used by IT professionals, system administrators, and network engineers to assess, analyze, and optimize the performance of computer systems, networks, applications, and services. These tools provide real-time visibility into system resources, application behavior, network traffic, and service availability, enabling administrators to identify performance bottlenecks, troubleshoot issues, and improve system efficiency, reliability, and user experience. Performance monitoring tools come in various forms, including software applications, command-line utilities, cloud-based services, and hardware appliances, each offering different features, capabilities, and deployment options to meet the diverse needs and requirements of organizations. One of the primary functions of performance monitoring tools is collecting and aggregating performance data from multiple sources, such as servers, network devices, databases, and applications, into centralized repositories or dashboards for analysis and visualization. Performance data may include metrics related to CPU usage, memory utilization, disk I/O, network throughput, application response times, server uptime, and error rates, among others, which are collected at regular intervals using monitoring agents, sensors, or probes deployed across the infrastructure. By consolidating performance data from disparate sources, performance monitoring tools provide administrators with a comprehensive view of system health, performance trends, and anomalies, enabling them to make informed decisions and take proactive measures to optimize system performance and mitigate performance issues. Another key function of performance monitoring tools is analyzing performance data to identify trends, patterns, and correlations that may indicate underlying performance issues or opportunities for optimization. Analytical features such as trend analysis, anomaly detection, correlation analysis, and predictive modeling enable administrators to identify deviations from normal behavior, detect performance bottlenecks, and forecast future performance trends based on historical data, helping them anticipate and address potential issues before they impact system performance or user experience. By leveraging advanced analytics and machine learning algorithms, performance monitoring tools can detect subtle performance patterns and anomalies that may go unnoticed by traditional monitoring approaches, enabling administrators to proactively identify and resolve issues that could affect system availability or performance. Additionally, performance monitoring tools provide visualization features, such as charts, graphs, dashboards, and heatmaps, that enable administrators to visualize performance data in meaningful and actionable ways, making it easier to identify trends, spot anomalies, and communicate insights to stakeholders effectively. Visualization tools allow administrators to customize dashboards, create performance reports, and drill down into specific metrics or dimensions to gain deeper insights into system behavior and performance trends, facilitating data-driven decision-making and collaboration across teams. By presenting performance data in a visually appealing and intuitive format, performance monitoring tools empower administrators to monitor system health, track performance metrics, and communicate performance insights to stakeholders in a clear and concise manner, fostering transparency, accountability, and alignment with business objectives. Furthermore, performance monitoring tools offer alerting and notification capabilities that enable administrators to set up thresholds, triggers, and rules to automatically detect and respond to performance issues in real time. Alerting features allow administrators to define thresholds for key performance metrics, such as CPU utilization, memory usage, or response times, and configure notifications to be triggered when performance metrics exceed predefined thresholds, indicating potential performance issues or service degradation. By receiving timely alerts and notifications, administrators can proactively investigate and remediate performance issues before they escalate into critical problems, minimizing downtime, and service disruptions, and preserving the integrity and availability of IT services. Moreover, performance monitoring tools often integrate with other IT management and monitoring solutions, such as configuration management databases (CMDBs), incident management systems, and service desk platforms, to streamline workflows, automate tasks, and facilitate cross-functional collaboration. Integration features enable administrators to correlate performance data with configuration data, event data, and incident records to gain deeper insights into the relationships between system configuration changes, performance events, and service disruptions, enabling them to make data-driven decisions and prioritize actions based on business impact and urgency. By integrating performance monitoring tools with other IT management systems, organizations can improve operational efficiency, accelerate incident resolution, and enhance the overall effectiveness of their IT operations. In summary, performance monitoring tools play a critical role in assessing, analyzing, and optimizing the performance of computer systems, networks, applications, and services. By collecting, analyzing, and visualizing performance data, identifying trends and anomalies, providing alerting and notification capabilities, and integrating with other IT management systems, performance monitoring tools empower administrators to monitor system health, detect performance issues, and optimize system performance proactively, ensuring the reliability, availability, and performance of IT services and infrastructure. Continual evaluation, selection, and deployment of performance monitoring tools are essential for organizations to adapt to evolving technology trends, business requirements, and performance challenges in today's dynamic and competitive IT landscape.

Optimization strategies for speed are essential techniques employed by software developers, system administrators, and IT professionals to improve the performance, responsiveness, and efficiency of computer systems, applications, and services, enabling faster execution, reduced latency, and enhanced user experience. These strategies encompass a wide range of approaches, including code optimization, algorithmic optimization, system configuration tuning, hardware upgrades, and caching techniques, each aimed at identifying and eliminating performance bottlenecks, reducing overhead, and maximizing resource utilization to achieve optimal speed and responsiveness. One of the fundamental optimization strategies for speed is code optimization, which involves analyzing and refining the source code of software applications to improve execution efficiency, reduce computational complexity, and minimize resource consumption. Code optimization techniques include eliminating redundant code, optimizing data structures and algorithms, reducing function call overhead, and leveraging compiler optimizations and language features to generate optimized machine code. By optimizing code for speed, developers can reduce the time required to execute critical code paths, improve overall application performance, and deliver a more responsive and seamless user experience. Additionally, algorithmic optimization is another essential strategy for improving speed, which involves selecting, designing, or modifying algorithms and data structures to minimize computational overhead, reduce time complexity, and improve scalability. Algorithmic optimization techniques include choosing the most efficient algorithms for specific tasks, optimizing algorithm parameters, parallelizing algorithms to leverage multicore processors, and implementing data structures optimized for fast access and retrieval. By optimizing algorithms and data structures, developers can accelerate the execution of computational tasks, reduce processing time, and improve application performance, especially for tasks involving large datasets or complex computations. Furthermore, system configuration tuning is a critical optimization strategy for improving speed, which involves adjusting system settings, parameters, and configurations to optimize resource utilization, mitigate contention, and reduce overhead. System configuration tuning techniques include adjusting CPU scheduling policies, memory allocation settings, disk I/O parameters, network buffer sizes, and operating system kernel parameters to optimize system performance and responsiveness. By tuning system configurations, administrators can minimize resource contention, reduce latency, and improve throughput, enabling faster response times and smoother operation of computer systems and applications. Moreover, hardware upgrades are an effective optimization strategy for enhancing speed, which involves replacing or upgrading hardware components, such as processors, memory modules, storage devices, and network interfaces, to increase computational power, memory capacity, storage bandwidth, and network throughput. Hardware upgrades can significantly improve system *performance, reduce latency, and enhance responsiveness, especially for compute-intensive, memory-intensive, or I/O-bound workloads. By investing in hardware upgrades, organizations can extend the lifespan of existing hardware infrastructure, accommodate growing workloads, and meet the performance demands of modern applications and services. Additionally, caching techniques are essential optimization strategies for improving speed, which involve storing frequently accessed data or computation results in fast-access memory or storage caches to reduce the latency of subsequent accesses and accelerate data retrieval. Caching techniques include using CPU caches, disk caches, database caches, and content delivery networks (CDNs) to cache data at various levels of the system hierarchy, such as the CPU, memory, disk, or network, depending on access patterns and performance requirements. By leveraging caching techniques, developers can reduce the time required to access and retrieve data, minimize network latency, and improve application responsiveness, resulting in faster load times and smoother user interactions. Furthermore, parallelization and concurrency are essential optimization strategies for improving speed, which involve dividing tasks into smaller subtasks and executing them concurrently on multiple processing units or threads to exploit parallelism and maximize throughput. Parallelization techniques include using multithreading, multiprocessing, task parallelism, and distributed computing frameworks to parallelize computations, I/O operations, and data processing tasks across multiple cores, processors, or nodes in a distributed system. By parallelizing workloads, developers can reduce execution time, improve scalability, and increase system throughput, enabling faster processing of large datasets, real-time analytics, and high-performance computing tasks. In summary, optimization strategies for speed are critical for improving the performance, responsiveness, and efficiency of computer systems, applications, and services. By employing code optimization, algorithmic optimization, system configuration tuning, hardware upgrades, caching techniques, parallelization, and concurrency, developers and administrators can identify and eliminate performance bottlenecks, reduce overhead, and maximize resource utilization to achieve optimal speed and responsiveness. Continual evaluation, testing, and refinement of optimization strategies are essential for organizations to adapt to evolving technology trends, workload requirements, and performance challenges in today's fast-paced and competitive IT landscape.*

Vulnerability assessment techniques are fundamental processes employed by cybersecurity professionals, system administrators, and IT teams to identify, analyze, and mitigate security vulnerabilities in computer systems, networks, and applications, safeguarding against potential security threats, data breaches, and cyberattacks. These techniques encompass a variety of methodologies, tools, and best practices aimed at systematically evaluating the security posture of IT assets, identifying weaknesses, and prioritizing remediation efforts to minimize risk and strengthen overall security defenses. One of the primary vulnerability assessment techniques is conducting vulnerability scans, which involves using automated scanning tools and software solutions to scan IT infrastructure, endpoints, and applications for known security vulnerabilities, misconfigurations, and weaknesses. Vulnerability scanning tools leverage databases of known vulnerabilities, such as the Common Vulnerabilities and Exposures (CVE) database, to identify software flaws, missing patches, insecure configurations, and other security issues that could be exploited by attackers. By performing regular vulnerability scans, organizations can detect and remediate security vulnerabilities proactively, reducing the likelihood of successful cyberattacks and data breaches. Additionally, penetration testing, also known as ethical hacking, is a critical vulnerability assessment technique that involves simulating real-world cyberattacks and exploitation techniques to assess the security of IT systems and applications. Penetration testers, or ethical hackers, use a combination of manual testing techniques, automated tools, and attack vectors to identify security vulnerabilities, exploit weaknesses, and gain unauthorized access to sensitive information or resources. By conducting penetration tests, organizations can identify critical security flaws, validate the effectiveness of security controls, and prioritize remediation efforts to improve overall security posture and resilience to cyber threats. Furthermore, vulnerability assessments often include web application security testing, which focuses on identifying vulnerabilities and security weaknesses in web applications, such as SQL injection, cross-site scripting (XSS), and insecure authentication mechanisms, that could be exploited by attackers to compromise sensitive data or perform unauthorized actions. Web application security testing involves using automated scanning tools, manual testing techniques, and source code analysis to identify and remediate security vulnerabilities in web applications, APIs, and web services, ensuring the integrity, confidentiality, and availability of web-based assets. By conducting comprehensive web application security testing, organizations can identify and address security vulnerabilities in web applications proactively, reducing the risk of data breaches and compliance violations.

Additionally, network security assessments are essential vulnerability assessment techniques that involve evaluating the security of network infrastructure, devices, and protocols to identify weaknesses, misconfigurations, and vulnerabilities that could be exploited by attackers to gain unauthorized access to networks, intercept sensitive data, or disrupt network operations. Network security assessments typically include network scanning, port scanning, vulnerability scanning, and configuration auditing to identify security vulnerabilities, unauthorized devices, and insecure network configurations, enabling organizations to strengthen network defenses and mitigate potential security risks. Moreover, social engineering assessments are critical vulnerability assessment techniques that involve testing the security awareness and resilience of employees, contractors, and stakeholders to social engineering attacks, such as phishing, pretexting, and social manipulation techniques, that exploit human psychology and trust to deceive individuals into disclosing sensitive information or performing unauthorized actions. Social engineering assessments typically include phishing simulations, social engineering audits, and security awareness training to educate users about common social engineering tactics, raise awareness of security risks, and empower individuals to recognize and report suspicious activities effectively. By conducting social engineering assessments, organizations can strengthen security awareness, enhance incident response capabilities, and mitigate the risk of social engineering attacks targeting personnel.

Additionally, vulnerability assessment techniques often include compliance audits and regulatory assessments, which involve evaluating organizational policies, procedures, and controls against industry standards, regulatory requirements, and best practices to ensure compliance with legal, contractual, and regulatory obligations. Compliance audits typically focus on assessing the effectiveness of security controls, risk management practices, and incident response procedures to identify gaps, deficiencies, and non-compliance issues that could expose organizations to legal liabilities, financial penalties, and reputational damage. By conducting regular compliance audits and regulatory assessments, organizations can ensure adherence to relevant standards, frameworks, and regulations, demonstrate due diligence, and mitigate the risk of regulatory violations and sanctions. In summary, vulnerability assessment techniques are essential processes for identifying, analyzing, and mitigating security vulnerabilities in computer systems, networks, and applications. By leveraging vulnerability scanning, penetration testing, web application security testing, network security assessments, social engineering assessments, compliance audits, and regulatory assessments, organizations can assess their security posture, identify weaknesses, and prioritize remediation efforts to strengthen overall security defenses and protect against cyber threats. Continual evaluation, testing, and refinement of vulnerability assessment techniques are essential for organizations to adapt to evolving cyber threats, security risks, and compliance requirements in today's dynamic and interconnected digital landscape.

Incident response and recovery are critical components of cybersecurity and IT operations, encompassing a set of procedures, processes, and practices designed to detect, respond to, and mitigate security incidents, breaches, and disruptions, and to restore affected systems, services, and data to normal operation efficiently. Incident response involves the coordinated effort of IT security teams, incident responders, and other stakeholders to identify, contain, eradicate, and recover from security incidents in a timely and effective manner, minimizing the impact on business operations, mitigating potential damage, and restoring trust and confidence in the organization's security posture. Incident response begins with incident detection, which involves monitoring IT infrastructure, systems, and networks for signs of security breaches, unusual activities, or anomalies that may indicate a security incident, such as unauthorized access attempts, malware infections, data exfiltration, or suspicious network traffic patterns. Incident detection techniques include security monitoring, log analysis, intrusion detection systems (IDS), intrusion prevention systems (IPS), antivirus software, and security information and event management (SIEM) solutions, which provide real-time visibility into security events, alerts, and anomalies, enabling organizations to detect and respond to security incidents promptly. Upon detection of a security incident, the next step in incident response is incident *triage and assessment, which involves evaluating the severity, scope, and impact of the incident, identifying affected assets, systems, and data, and determining the appropriate response actions and escalation procedures based on the organization's incident response plan, policies, and procedures. Incident triage and assessment enable organizations to prioritize incident response efforts, allocate resources effectively, and initiate containment and mitigation measures to prevent further damage and disruption to business operations. Additionally, incident response includes incident containment, which involves isolating and quarantining affected systems, endpoints, or network segments to prevent the spread of the incident, limit its impact, and preserve forensic evidence for investigation and analysis. Incident containment measures may include disabling compromised accounts, disconnecting infected devices from the network, blocking malicious traffic, and implementing access controls and firewall rules to contain the incident and prevent unauthorized access or data loss. By containing the incident promptly, organizations can minimize the scope of the incident, reduce the risk of further damage, and facilitate the recovery and restoration of affected systems and services. Moreover, incident response encompasses incident eradication, which involves removing the root cause of the incident, eliminating malicious actors or malware from affected systems, and remediating vulnerabilities or weaknesses exploited by the incident to prevent recurrence. Incident eradication measures may include applying security patches and updates, removing malware infections, restoring system configurations from backups, and implementing security best practices and controls to strengthen defenses and prevent similar incidents in the future. By eradicating the incident thoroughly and addressing underlying security weaknesses, organizations can prevent repeat incidents, improve security posture, and enhance resilience to cyber threats and attacks. Additionally, incident response includes incident recovery, which involves restoring affected systems, services, and data to normal operation, minimizing downtime, and restoring business continuity and productivity. Incident recovery measures may include restoring data from backups, rebuilding compromised systems, verifying system integrity, and conducting post-incident analysis and testing to ensure the effectiveness of recovery efforts. By prioritizing incident recovery and restoring critical services promptly, organizations can minimize the impact of the incident on business operations, mitigate financial losses, and preserve customer trust and confidence. Furthermore, incident response encompasses post-incident analysis and lessons learned, which involves reviewing and analyzing the incident response process, identifying strengths, weaknesses, and areas for improvement, and documenting lessons learned and best practices for future incidents. Post-incident analysis enables organizations to identify root causes of incidents, evaluate the effectiveness of incident response procedures and controls, and implement corrective actions and improvements to enhance incident response capabilities and resilience. By learning from past incidents and continuously improving incident response processes and procedures, organizations can better prepare for future incidents, respond more effectively to emerging threats, and mitigate the risk of security breaches and disruptions. Moreover, incident response includes communication and coordination, which involves notifying stakeholders, partners, regulators, and law enforcement agencies about the incident, providing timely updates and status reports, and coordinating response efforts across internal teams and external organizations to ensure a unified and coordinated response. Effective communication and coordination are essential for maintaining transparency, managing expectations, and facilitating collaboration and cooperation among all parties involved in incident response and recovery efforts. By establishing clear lines of communication, defining roles and responsibilities, and fostering collaboration and teamwork, organizations can streamline incident response efforts, minimize confusion and misunderstandings, and facilitate the timely resolution of security incidents. In summary, incident response and recovery are essential processes for mitigating the impact of security incidents, breaches, and disruptions, restoring normal operations, and maintaining the integrity, availability, and confidentiality of IT systems, services, and data. By implementing effective incident response plans, procedures, and practices, organizations can detect and respond to security incidents promptly, minimize the impact on business operations, and enhance resilience to cyber threats and attacks. Continual evaluation, testing, and refinement of incident response capabilities are essential for organizations to adapt to evolving security threats, regulatory requirements, and business needs in today's dynamic and interconnected digital landscape.*

Data reconstruction techniques are fundamental processes utilized in data recovery and forensic investigations to reconstruct, recover, and restore lost, damaged, or corrupted data from storage devices, such as hard drives, solid-state drives (SSDs), USB drives, and memory cards, to ensure data integrity, availability, and usability. These techniques encompass a variety of methods, tools, and algorithms aimed at recovering lost or inaccessible data due to accidental deletion, formatting, file system corruption, hardware failures, or malicious activities, enabling organizations and individuals to retrieve valuable information and restore critical data assets effectively. One of the primary data reconstruction techniques is file carving, which involves extracting and reconstructing files and data fragments from storage media based on file signatures, headers, footers, and metadata, without relying on file system structures or metadata information. File carving techniques use advanced algorithms and pattern matching mechanisms to identify and recover file types, such as documents, images, videos, and archives, from raw disk images or fragmented storage media, enabling forensic investigators and data recovery specialists to retrieve deleted or damaged files, even when file system structures are corrupted or inaccessible. By employing file carving techniques, organizations can recover critical files and documents lost due to accidental deletion, file system corruption, or disk errors, preserving data integrity and minimizing data loss in forensic investigations or data recovery scenarios. Additionally, data reconstruction techniques often include file system analysis and repair, which involves analyzing the structure and integrity of file systems, such as FAT, NTFS, exFAT, and HFS+, and repairing or rebuilding file system metadata, directory structures, and file allocation tables to restore access to lost or damaged files and directories. File system analysis tools, such as fsck (file system check), chkdsk (check disk), and TestDisk, scan storage devices for file system inconsistencies, errors, and corruption, and attempt to repair file system structures, recover lost partitions, and rebuild directory hierarchies to facilitate data recovery and file system repair. By performing file system analysis and repair, organizations can recover data from corrupt or damaged file systems, restore file system integrity, and ensure the availability and usability of critical data assets. Moreover, data reconstruction techniques include disk imaging and cloning, which involve creating exact replicas or disk images of storage devices, including hard drives, SSDs, and removable media, to preserve data integrity, facilitate data recovery, and prevent further data loss during forensic investigations or data recovery operations. Disk imaging tools, such as dd (disk dump) and ddrescue, create bit-by-bit copies of storage devices, including all data sectors, partitions, and file system structures, enabling investigators and recovery specialists to analyze, recover, and restore data from disk images without risking further damage to original storage media. By creating disk images and clones, organizations can preserve evidence, facilitate forensic analysis, and recover lost or damaged data in a controlled and non-destructive manner, ensuring data integrity and minimizing the risk of data loss or corruption. Additionally, data reconstruction techniques often include data carving and file system journal analysis, which involve extracting and reconstructing data fragments and files from storage media by analyzing file system journals, transaction logs, and unallocated disk space, where deleted or lost data may reside. Data carving tools, such as Foremost, Scalpel, and Photorec, scan disk images or raw storage media for file signatures, file headers, and data patterns, and extract files and data fragments based on predefined file formats and criteria, enabling investigators to recover deleted files, hidden data, and remnants of deleted or damaged files from storage media. By employing data carving and file system journal analysis techniques, organizations can recover valuable data from inaccessible or damaged storage media, reconstruct deleted files, and preserve evidence for forensic investigations and legal proceedings. Furthermore, data reconstruction techniques often involve RAID data recovery and reconstruction, which involve recovering data from redundant array of independent disks (RAID) configurations, such as RAID 0, RAID 1, RAID 5, and RAID 6, in the event of disk failures, controller errors, or RAID array corruption. RAID data recovery tools and techniques use parity information, redundant data, and RAID algorithms to rebuild missing or damaged data blocks, reconstruct RAID arrays, and recover lost or inaccessible data from RAID volumes, ensuring data availability and integrity in RAID environments. By performing RAID data recovery and reconstruction, organizations can minimize downtime, restore critical data assets, and maintain business continuity in the event of RAID failures or data corruption incidents. In summary, data reconstruction techniques are essential processes for recovering lost, damaged, or corrupted data from storage devices, ensuring data integrity, availability, and usability in forensic investigations, data recovery operations, and disaster recovery scenarios. By employing file carving, file system analysis, disk imaging, data carving, RAID data recovery, and other data reconstruction techniques, organizations can recover valuable data assets, preserve evidence, and mitigate the impact of data loss or corruption incidents effectively. Continual evaluation, testing, and refinement of data reconstruction techniques are essential for organizations to adapt to evolving data recovery challenges, technology trends, and security threats in today's dynamic and interconnected digital landscape.

Recovery from disk failures is a crucial aspect of data management and IT operations, involving processes, strategies, and techniques aimed at restoring data integrity, availability, and continuity in the event of disk hardware failures, malfunctions, or errors. Disk failures can occur due to various reasons, including mechanical failures, electronic failures, firmware issues, logical errors, and natural disasters, posing significant risks to data loss, downtime, and business operations. Therefore, organizations implement robust disk recovery strategies and procedures to mitigate the impact of disk failures, minimize data loss, and ensure business continuity. One of the primary approaches to recovery from disk failures is data redundancy, which involves implementing redundant storage configurations, such as RAID (Redundant Array of Independent Disks), to distribute data across multiple disks, maintain data redundancy, and enable fault tolerance in the event of disk failures. RAID configurations, such as RAID 1 (mirroring), RAID 5 (striping with parity), and RAID 6 (striping with double parity), use disk redundancy and parity information to protect against disk failures, allowing data to be reconstructed and recovered from failed disks without data loss. By implementing RAID configurations, organizations can mitigate the risk of data loss due to disk failures, ensure continuous access to critical data, and maintain business operations even in the presence of disk hardware failures. Additionally, organizations employ disk monitoring and predictive maintenance techniques to proactively monitor the health, performance, and reliability of disk drives, identify early warning signs of disk failures, and take preemptive actions to prevent data loss and minimize downtime. Disk monitoring tools and utilities, such as SMART (Self-Monitoring, Analysis, and Reporting Technology), disk health diagnostics, and predictive analytics algorithms, analyze disk drive metrics, error rates, and performance indicators to assess disk health and predict potential failures before they occur. By *monitoring disk health and performance, organizations can identify failing disks, initiate disk replacement procedures, and migrate data to healthy disks to prevent data loss and maintain service availability. Furthermore, organizations implement backup and disaster recovery (DR) strategies to create copies of critical data and applications, store them in offsite locations or cloud environments, and facilitate data recovery and restoration in the event of disk failures, data corruption, or catastrophic events. Backup and DR strategies involve regular data backups, data replication, snapshotting, and continuous data protection (CDP) techniques to create point-in-time copies of data, which can be used to restore data to a previous state in case of disk failures or data loss incidents. By implementing backup and DR strategies, organizations can ensure data resilience, minimize the impact of disk failures, and recover critical data and applications quickly to resume business operations and minimize downtime. Additionally, organizations utilize disk repair and recovery tools and software solutions to diagnose, repair, and recover data from failed or corrupted disk drives, including hard disk drives (HDDs), solid-state drives (SSDs), and external storage devices. Disk repair and recovery tools, such as disk repair utilities, data recovery software, and disk imaging solutions, scan disk drives for errors, bad sectors, and file system corruption, and attempt to repair disk errors, recover lost data, and restore disk functionality to facilitate data recovery and disk repair operations. By employing disk repair and recovery tools, organizations* can recover valuable data from failed disks, minimize data loss, and restore disk functionality to mitigate the impact of disk failures on business operations. Moreover, organizations implement disk redundancy and fault-tolerant storage architectures, such as storage area networks (SANs), network-attached storage (NAS), and distributed file systems, to distribute data across multiple storage nodes, ensure data availability, and enable data recovery in the event of disk failures or storage node failures. These storage architectures use redundancy, data replication, and data mirroring techniques to replicate data across multiple storage devices, eliminate single points of failure, and maintain data availability and integrity in the face of disk hardware failures, network outages, or storage subsystem failures. By implementing fault-tolerant storage architectures, organizations can minimize the impact of disk failures, ensure continuous access to critical data, and maintain service availability for users and applications. Furthermore, organizations leverage disk cloning and imaging techniques to create exact replicas or images of disk drives, partitions, or entire storage volumes, enabling them to duplicate data, migrate data between storage devices, and recover data from failed disks or corrupted file systems. Disk cloning and imaging tools, such as dd (disk dump), Clonezilla, and Acronis True Image, create sector-by-sector copies of disk drives or partitions, including all data, partitions, and file system structures, allowing organizations to preserve data integrity, facilitate data recovery, and restore data to replacement disks or storage devices *efficiently. By utilizing disk cloning and imaging techniques, organizations can simplify data migration, streamline disk replacement procedures, and expedite data recovery operations to minimize downtime and ensure business continuity in the face of disk failures. In summary, recovery from disk failures is a critical aspect of data management and IT operations, involving proactive strategies, tools, and techniques to mitigate the impact of disk hardware failures, minimize data loss, and ensure business continuity. By implementing disk redundancy, monitoring disk health, backup and disaster recovery, disk repair and recovery, fault-tolerant storage architectures, disk cloning and imaging, organizations can effectively recover from disk failures, maintain data availability, and protect critical data assets from loss or corruption. Continual evaluation, testing, and refinement of disk recovery strategies and procedures are essential for organizations to adapt to evolving technology trends, storage challenges, and business requirements in today's dynamic and data-driven digital landscape.*

Troubleshooting virtual machine (VM) issues is a critical aspect of managing virtualized environments, involving the identification, diagnosis, and resolution of problems that affect the performance, stability, and availability of virtual machines and the applications and services they host. Virtualization technology enables organizations to maximize resource utilization, improve scalability, and streamline IT operations by running multiple virtual machines on a single physical server or host system, but it also introduces unique challenges and complexities that require effective troubleshooting techniques and strategies to address. One common issue encountered when troubleshooting virtual machines is performance degradation, which can manifest as slow response times, high resource utilization, or latency issues within the virtualized environment. Performance degradation in virtual machines can be caused by various factors, including resource contention, overcommitment of resources, misconfigured virtual machine settings, or inefficient resource allocation. Troubleshooting performance issues often involves identifying resource bottlenecks, analyzing performance metrics, and optimizing resource allocation to improve virtual machine performance and responsiveness. Additionally, virtual machine crashes or unresponsiveness may occur due to software bugs, driver issues, or incompatible hardware configurations, leading to downtime and service disruptions. Troubleshooting virtual machine crashes typically involves analyzing system logs, crash dumps, and error messages to identify the underlying cause of the crash, applying software updates or patches, and ensuring compatibility with hypervisor software and hardware components. Furthermore, network connectivity problems can arise in virtualized environments, affecting communication between virtual machines, external networks, and network services. Network troubleshooting in virtual machines involves verifying network configurations, checking network connectivity, and diagnosing network traffic issues using tools such as ping, traceroute, and network packet captures. Resolving network connectivity problems may require adjusting firewall rules, updating network drivers, or configuring virtual network interfaces to ensure proper communication between virtual machines and network resources. Another common issue when troubleshooting virtual machines is disk space and storage-related problems, such as insufficient disk space, disk performance issues, or disk corruption. Troubleshooting disk space issues involves monitoring disk usage, identifying large or unnecessary files, and performing disk cleanup operations to free up storage space. Additionally, disk performance issues may require optimizing disk I/O operations, adjusting storage configurations, or upgrading storage hardware to improve disk performance and responsiveness. Moreover, virtual machine snapshots can sometimes cause storage-related problems, such as increased disk space usage, performance degradation, or snapshot *corruption. Troubleshooting snapshot issues involves monitoring snapshot usage, managing snapshot lifecycles, and consolidating or deleting unnecessary snapshots to reclaim storage space and improve virtual machine performance. Furthermore, security vulnerabilities and compliance issues can arise in virtualized environments, posing risks to sensitive data, applications, and virtual machine instances. Troubleshooting security vulnerabilities involves implementing security best practices, applying security patches and updates, and conducting security audits and vulnerability assessments to identify and remediate security weaknesses in virtualized environments. Additionally, compliance issues may arise due to misconfiguration, improper access controls, or unauthorized changes to virtual machine configurations. Troubleshooting compliance issues involves ensuring adherence to regulatory requirements, industry standards, and organizational policies, and implementing controls and safeguards to maintain compliance in virtualized environments. Moreover, virtual machine migration and live migration failures can occur when transferring virtual machines between host systems or data centers, leading to service disruptions and downtime. Troubleshooting migration issues involves diagnosing migration errors, verifying network connectivity, and ensuring compatibility between source and destination host systems. Resolving migration failures may require adjusting migration settings, troubleshooting network issues, or addressing compatibility issues with hypervisor software and hardware components. Additionally, troubleshooting resource allocation and contention issues is essential for optimizing resource utilization and performance in virtualized environments. Resource allocation problems may arise due to overprovisioning or underprovisioning of resources, leading to performance bottlenecks, resource contention, or inefficient resource utilization. Troubleshooting resource allocation issues involves analyzing resource utilization metrics, adjusting resource allocations, and optimizing workload placement to ensure optimal performance and resource utilization in virtualized environments. Moreover, troubleshooting virtual machine backups and disaster recovery processes is crucial for ensuring data protection and business continuity in virtualized environments. Backup and recovery failures can occur due to backup software errors, storage problems, or configuration issues, leading to data loss or data corruption. Troubleshooting backup and recovery issues involves verifying backup configurations, testing backup and recovery processes, and ensuring data integrity and recoverability in virtualized environments. Additionally, troubleshooting compatibility issues between virtual machines and hypervisor software, guest operating systems, or applications is essential for ensuring interoperability and performance in virtualized environments. Compatibility problems may arise due to software bugs, driver issues, or incompatibilities between different software versions or components. Troubleshooting compatibility issues involves identifying compatibility issues, applying software updates or patches, and ensuring compatibility between virtualized components to maintain stability and performance in virtualized environments. In summary, troubleshooting virtual machine issues requires a systematic approach to identify, diagnose, and resolve problems affecting the performance, stability, and availability of virtualized environments. By understanding common virtual machine issues and employing effective troubleshooting techniques and strategies, organizations can minimize downtime, optimize resource utilization, and ensure the reliability and performance of virtualized environments in today's dynamic and evolving IT landscape. Continual evaluation, testing, and refinement of troubleshooting processes are essential for organizations to adapt to changing technology trends, business requirements, and security threats in virtualized environments. Cloud service outage resolution is a critical aspect of managing cloud-based services and infrastructure, involving processes, procedures, and strategies aimed at identifying, diagnosing, and resolving service disruptions, downtime, and performance issues affecting cloud-based applications, platforms, and services. Cloud service outages can occur due to various factors, including hardware failures, software bugs, network issues, data center disruptions, human errors, cyberattacks, or unexpected events, posing significant risks to business continuity, data integrity, and service availability. Therefore, organizations implement robust outage resolution strategies and incident response procedures to minimize the impact of cloud service outages, restore service functionality, and ensure uninterrupted access to critical business applications and data. One of the primary approaches to cloud service outage resolution is proactive monitoring and alerting, which involves continuously monitoring cloud-based infrastructure, applications, and services for performance anomalies, errors, or service disruptions using monitoring tools, agents, and sensors. Proactive monitoring enables organizations to detect potential issues or abnormalities in real-time, trigger alerts or notifications to IT teams or administrators, and initiate incident response procedures promptly to investigate and resolve service outages before they impact end-users or business operations. Additionally, organizations leverage cloud service status dashboards, service health portals, and communication channels provided by cloud service providers to stay informed about service status, availability, and incidents, and to receive timely updates and notifications about ongoing service outages or disruptions. By staying proactive and informed, organizations can expedite the resolution of cloud service outages, minimize downtime, and maintain service availability and reliability for users and customers. Moreover, cloud service outage resolution involves incident response and escalation procedures, which outline the steps, roles, and responsibilities for IT teams and stakeholders to follow when responding to cloud service incidents, such as service disruptions, performance degradation, or availability issues. Incident response procedures typically include steps for incident detection, triage, investigation, resolution, and post-incident analysis, as well as escalation paths and communication protocols to notify management, stakeholders, and customers about the incident status, impact, and resolution progress. By establishing clear incident response procedures and escalation paths, organizations can streamline outage resolution efforts, facilitate coordination and collaboration among IT teams, and ensure timely resolution of cloud service incidents to minimize the impact on business operations and customer satisfaction. Additionally, organizations implement redundancy and failover mechanisms to enhance service availability and resilience in the event of cloud service outages or disruptions. Redundancy and failover mechanisms involve deploying redundant components, such as redundant servers, storage, networking, or data centers, and configuring automatic failover mechanisms to reroute traffic or workload to redundant components or backup systems when primary systems or services become unavailable. By implementing redundancy and failover mechanisms, organizations can mitigate the impact of cloud service outages, maintain service continuity, and ensure uninterrupted access to critical applications and data for users and customers. Furthermore, cloud service outage resolution involves root cause analysis (RCA) and post-incident analysis, which involve investigating the underlying causes of service outages, identifying contributing factors or weaknesses in cloud infrastructure or configurations, and implementing corrective actions or preventive measures to prevent recurrence. RCA and post-incident analysis enable organizations to learn from service outages, improve incident response processes, and enhance the resilience and reliability of cloud-based services and infrastructure. By conducting thorough RCA and post-incident analysis, organizations can identify opportunities for optimization, strengthen security controls, and implement best practices to mitigate the risk of future service outages or disruptions. Additionally, cloud service outage resolution involves communication and transparency, which are essential for maintaining trust and confidence among stakeholders, customers, and users during service disruptions or downtime. Effective communication involves timely updates, status reports, and incident notifications to inform stakeholders about the incident impact, resolution progress, and expected time to resolution, as well as proactive communication about preventive measures, service improvements, and lessons learned from service outages. By fostering transparency and open communication, organizations can demonstrate accountability, manage expectations, and mitigate reputational damage during cloud service outages or disruptions. Moreover, organizations leverage cloud service level agreements (SLAs), contracts, and vendor relationships to establish service expectations, performance metrics, and escalation procedures with cloud service providers, and to hold providers accountable for meeting service availability, uptime, and performance targets. Cloud SLAs typically include provisions for outage resolution, service credits, and compensation mechanisms in the event of service disruptions or downtime exceeding agreed-upon thresholds. By negotiating SLAs and contracts with cloud service providers, organizations can ensure contractual protections, service guarantees, and recourse options in the event of cloud service outages or performance issues. In summary, cloud service outage resolution is a multifaceted process that requires proactive monitoring, incident response, redundancy, RCA, communication, and SLA management to minimize the impact of service disruptions, restore service functionality, and ensure business continuity in cloud-based environments. By implementing robust outage resolution strategies and procedures, organizations can mitigate the risk of cloud service outages, maintain service availability and reliability, and deliver seamless and uninterrupted access to critical applications and data for users and customers. Continual evaluation, testing, and refinement of outage resolution processes are essential for organizations to adapt to evolving technology trends, cloud service challenges, and business requirements in today's dynamic and interconnected digital landscape.*

Scripting for troubleshooting automation is an essential aspect of modern IT operations, enabling organizations to streamline and enhance the efficiency of their troubleshooting processes by automating repetitive tasks, executing predefined actions, and analyzing system data programmatically. Scripting languages such as Python, PowerShell, Bash, and Perl provide powerful tools and frameworks for creating scripts that automate various aspects of troubleshooting, from system monitoring and log analysis to configuration management and remediation. By leveraging scripting for troubleshooting automation, organizations can reduce manual intervention, accelerate problem resolution, and improve overall system reliability and performance. One of the key benefits of scripting for troubleshooting automation is the ability to automate routine tasks and procedures, such as system checks, log parsing, and error detection, which would otherwise require manual effort and intervention. For example, organizations can use scripts to monitor system resources, such as CPU usage, memory utilization, and disk space, and trigger alerts or actions when predefined thresholds are exceeded, allowing IT teams to proactively address potential issues before they impact system performance or availability. Moreover, scripting enables organizations to automate the analysis of system logs, event data, and diagnostic information, allowing IT teams to quickly identify and diagnose problems, such as application errors, configuration issues, or security incidents, and take appropriate remedial actions to resolve them. By automating log analysis and troubleshooting processes, organizations can minimize downtime, reduce mean time to resolution (MTTR), and improve the overall reliability and availability of their IT infrastructure. Additionally, scripting for troubleshooting automation enables organizations to implement proactive maintenance and remediation strategies, such as automated patch management, software updates, and configuration changes, to ensure system security, compliance, and performance. For example, organizations can use scripts to automate the deployment of security patches and updates across their IT infrastructure, ensuring that systems are protected against known vulnerabilities and security threats. Similarly, scripts can be used to automate configuration changes and updates, such as firewall rules, network settings, and application configurations, allowing organizations to enforce standardized configurations, reduce human errors, and maintain system integrity and consistency. Furthermore, scripting facilitates the integration and orchestration of disparate IT systems, tools, and technologies, enabling organizations to create end-to-end automation workflows that span across multiple systems and platforms. For example, organizations can use scripts to integrate monitoring systems with ticketing systems, enabling automated incident ticketing and workflow orchestration based on predefined triggers and conditions. Similarly, scripts can be used to integrate configuration management tools with version control systems, allowing automated deployment and rollback of configuration changes across development, testing, and production environments. By orchestrating workflows and integrating systems through scripting, organizations can streamline IT operations, improve collaboration between teams, and accelerate the delivery of IT services and solutions. Moreover, scripting for troubleshooting automation enables organizations to scale their IT operations and infrastructure efficiently, allowing them to manage growing complexity, volume, and diversity of IT environments and workloads. For example, organizations can use scripts to automate the provisioning and deployment of virtual machines, containers, and cloud resources, enabling rapid scaling and elasticity in response to changing business demands and workloads. Similarly, scripts can be used to automate resource allocation and optimization, such as workload balancing, resource pooling, and auto-scaling, allowing organizations to maximize resource utilization, minimize costs, and improve overall efficiency and agility. Additionally, scripting empowers IT teams to create custom solutions and tools tailored to their specific needs and requirements, allowing them to address unique challenges and scenarios that off-the-shelf products and solutions may not adequately support. For example, organizations can develop custom scripts to automate niche tasks and processes, such as data migration, legacy system integration, or *compliance auditing, allowing them to achieve greater flexibility, control, and efficiency in their IT operations. Furthermore, scripting fosters innovation and experimentation within IT teams, encouraging collaboration, knowledge sharing, and continuous improvement in troubleshooting and automation practices. By empowering IT professionals to develop and share scripts, tools, and best practices, organizations can foster a culture of innovation and agility, enabling them to adapt to evolving technology trends, business requirements, and industry standards. In summary, scripting for troubleshooting automation is a valuable tool and approach that enables organizations to enhance the efficiency, reliability, and scalability of their IT operations by automating routine tasks, streamlining troubleshooting processes, and improving overall system performance and resilience. By leveraging scripting languages and frameworks, organizations can automate log analysis, system monitoring, configuration management, and remediation tasks, enabling them to minimize downtime, reduce human errors, and improve the agility and responsiveness of their IT infrastructure. Continual investment in scripting skills, tools, and best practices is essential for organizations to realize the full potential of scripting for troubleshooting automation and stay ahead in today's fast-paced and competitive digital landscape.*

Implementing monitoring and alerting systems is a fundamental aspect of modern IT infrastructure management, providing organizations with the capability to proactively monitor, track, and manage the health, performance, and availability of their IT resources, applications, and services in real-time. Monitoring and alerting systems play a critical role in ensuring the reliability, stability, and security of IT environments by detecting anomalies, identifying potential issues, and triggering alerts or notifications to IT teams or administrators for timely intervention and resolution. One of the primary objectives of implementing monitoring and alerting systems is to gain visibility into the performance and behavior of IT infrastructure components, including servers, networks, databases, applications, and cloud services, to ensure optimal operation and prevent downtime or service disruptions. By monitoring key performance indicators (KPIs), such as CPU usage, memory utilization, disk I/O, network latency, and application response times, organizations can identify performance bottlenecks, capacity constraints, or resource contention issues that may impact system performance or user experience. Additionally, monitoring and alerting systems enable organizations to track service-level agreements (SLAs), performance targets, and uptime guarantees, allowing them to measure, report, and enforce service availability and reliability commitments to customers, stakeholders, and end-users. Moreover, implementing monitoring and alerting systems facilitates proactive problem detection and troubleshooting, enabling IT teams to identify and address potential issues before they escalate into service outages or performance degradation. By setting up predefined thresholds, baselines, and alerting rules, organizations can configure monitoring systems to trigger alerts or notifications when certain conditions or events occur, such as exceeding resource thresholds, reaching capacity limits, or encountering error conditions, enabling IT teams to respond promptly and mitigate risks to service availability and performance. Furthermore, monitoring and alerting systems enable organizations to automate incident detection, triage, and response processes, allowing them to streamline incident management workflows, reduce mean time to resolution (MTTR), and improve overall operational efficiency and service quality. By integrating monitoring systems with incident management tools, ticketing systems, and communication platforms, organizations can automate the creation, assignment, and tracking of incidents, notify relevant stakeholders or teams about incident status and updates, and facilitate collaboration and coordination among IT teams for faster problem resolution and service restoration. Additionally, implementing monitoring and alerting systems supports capacity planning, performance optimization, and resource allocation decisions by providing organizations with valuable insights into usage trends, workload patterns, and resource utilization metrics. By analyzing historical performance data, forecasting future demand, and identifying potential capacity constraints or performance bottlenecks, organizations can optimize resource allocation, scale infrastructure proactively, and ensure adequate capacity to support business growth and evolving workloads. Moreover, monitoring and alerting systems enable organizations to enhance security posture and threat detection capabilities by monitoring for suspicious activities, unauthorized access attempts, or security breaches across IT environments. By correlating security events, analyzing log data, and detecting anomalous behavior patterns, organizations can identify potential security incidents, respond promptly to security threats, and strengthen their overall cybersecurity defenses to protect sensitive data, applications, and infrastructure from malicious actors or cyberattacks. Additionally, implementing monitoring and alerting systems fosters a culture of accountability, transparency, and continuous improvement within organizations by providing stakeholders, management, and IT teams with visibility into system performance, operational metrics, and service quality metrics. By sharing performance data, incident reports, and trend analysis with stakeholders, organizations can demonstrate adherence to service level agreements (SLAs), compliance requirements, and industry standards, and drive continuous improvement initiatives to optimize IT operations, enhance service delivery, and meet business objectives. Furthermore, implementing monitoring and alerting systems enables organizations to leverage advanced analytics, machine learning, and artificial intelligence (AI) technologies to enhance monitoring capabilities, automate anomaly detection, and predict potential issues or failures before they occur. By applying predictive analytics algorithms to historical performance data, organizations can identify patterns, trends, and anomalies indicative of impending failures or degraded performance, enabling them to take proactive measures to prevent downtime, optimize resource utilization, and maintain service availability and reliability. In summary, implementing monitoring and alerting systems is essential for organizations to ensure the reliability, availability, and performance of their IT infrastructure, applications, and services in today's dynamic and fast-paced digital landscape. By leveraging monitoring and alerting systems, organizations can gain visibility into system performance, detect potential issues, and respond promptly to incidents or anomalies, enabling them to minimize downtime, improve service quality, and enhance overall operational efficiency and customer satisfaction. Continual investment in monitoring technologies, best practices, and process improvements is essential for organizations to stay ahead of evolving technology trends, business requirements, and security threats and maintain a competitive edge in today's increasingly digital and interconnected world.

*Real-world troubleshooting examples provide invaluable
insights into practical problem-solving techniques,
methodologies, and best practices that IT professionals
can apply to address a wide range of issues and
challenges encountered in real-life IT environments. By
examining real-world troubleshooting scenarios and
case studies, IT professionals gain firsthand knowledge
and experience of how to diagnose, troubleshoot, and
resolve common and complex issues effectively and
efficiently. Real-world troubleshooting examples
encompass a diverse range of IT disciplines, including
network troubleshooting, system administration,
software debugging, cybersecurity incident response,
hardware diagnostics, and cloud service management,
reflecting the multifaceted nature of modern IT
operations and infrastructure. These examples often
illustrate the importance of systematic troubleshooting
approaches, such as gathering information, identifying
symptoms, isolating root causes, testing hypotheses,
and implementing solutions, to effectively address IT
issues and restore service functionality. For instance, in
a network troubleshooting scenario, IT professionals
may encounter connectivity issues between network
devices, such as switches, routers, and servers, affecting
communication and data transfer across the network.
By analyzing network diagrams, examining*

configuration files, and performing network tests, IT professionals can identify misconfigured settings, routing issues, or hardware failures that may be causing the connectivity problem and take corrective actions to restore network connectivity and functionality. Similarly, in a system administration scenario, IT professionals may encounter performance degradation or system crashes on critical servers or applications, impacting user productivity and business operations. By analyzing system logs, monitoring performance metrics, and conducting system diagnostics, IT professionals can identify resource bottlenecks, software bugs, or configuration errors that may be causing the performance issues and implement remedial measures, such as optimizing system settings, applying software patches, or reallocating resources, to improve system stability and performance. Moreover, real-world troubleshooting examples provide valuable insights into the importance of collaboration, communication, and teamwork in resolving IT issues effectively and efficiently. In complex troubleshooting scenarios involving multiple systems, technologies, or teams, effective communication and collaboration are essential for sharing information, coordinating efforts, and leveraging collective expertise to diagnose and resolve issues collaboratively. By fostering a collaborative troubleshooting culture and establishing clear communication channels and escalation paths, organizations can facilitate knowledge sharing, skill development, and problem-solving capabilities among IT teams, enabling them to respond more effectively to IT issues and challenges as they arise. Additionally, real-world troubleshooting examples highlight the importance of documentation, knowledge management, and lessons learned in building organizational resilience and improving troubleshooting capabilities over time. By documenting troubleshooting processes, solutions, and outcomes, organizations can capture valuable insights, best practices, and lessons learned from past experiences, enabling IT teams to leverage this knowledge to address similar issues more efficiently in the future. Furthermore, real-world troubleshooting examples underscore the need for continuous learning, training, and professional development among IT professionals to stay abreast of evolving technologies, methodologies, and best practices in troubleshooting and IT operations. By investing in ongoing training programs, certifications, and skill development initiatives, organizations can empower IT professionals with the knowledge, tools, and expertise needed to tackle increasingly complex IT challenges and deliver superior service and support to users and customers. In summary, real-world troubleshooting examples play a crucial role in enhancing the problem-solving skills, expertise, and confidence of IT professionals, enabling them to effectively diagnose, troubleshoot, and resolve a wide range of IT issues and challenges encountered in real-life environments. By studying real-world troubleshooting scenarios and case studies, IT professionals gain practical insights, techniques, and strategies for addressing common and complex IT issues, improving service reliability, and enhancing user satisfaction. Continual exposure to real-world troubleshooting examples, coupled with ongoing training and professional development, empowers IT professionals with the knowledge, skills, and capabilities needed to navigate the complexities of modern IT environments and deliver value-added solutions and services to organizations in today's rapidly evolving digital landscape.

Analyzing troubleshooting successes and failures is an essential practice for IT professionals and organizations seeking to improve their problem-solving capabilities, enhance service reliability, and optimize IT operations. By examining past troubleshooting experiences, both successful and unsuccessful, IT teams can identify patterns, trends, and lessons learned that inform future troubleshooting efforts and contribute to continuous improvement and innovation. Successful troubleshooting outcomes provide valuable insights into effective problem-solving techniques, methodologies, and best practices that IT professionals can replicate and build upon in similar situations. Conversely, failures offer critical learning opportunities by highlighting areas for improvement, uncovering gaps in knowledge or skills, and identifying systemic issues or root causes that may have contributed to the failure. Through systematic analysis and reflection on both successes and failures, IT professionals can refine their troubleshooting approaches, strengthen their problem-solving skills, and enhance their ability to address a wide range of IT issues and challenges effectively. One of the key aspects of analyzing troubleshooting successes is identifying the factors and strategies that contributed to the successful resolution of the issue. This may include identifying the root cause of the problem, leveraging diagnostic tools and techniques effectively, collaborating with team members or subject matter experts, following established troubleshooting methodologies, and implementing appropriate solutions or workarounds in a timely manner. By identifying and documenting the key factors that contributed to success, IT professionals can establish best practices, standard operating procedures, and guidelines for future troubleshooting efforts, enabling them to replicate successful outcomes and improve overall service reliability and user satisfaction. Additionally, analyzing successful troubleshooting outcomes enables organizations to recognize and celebrate the achievements and contributions of IT teams, fostering a culture of recognition, appreciation, and continuous improvement within the organization. Conversely, analyzing troubleshooting failures requires a candid and introspective examination of the factors, decisions, and actions that led to the unsuccessful resolution of the issue. This may involve identifying gaps in knowledge, skills, or resources, assessing the effectiveness of troubleshooting techniques or methodologies used, evaluating the accuracy and relevance of diagnostic data or information gathered, and identifying any communication or coordination issues that may have hindered the troubleshooting process. By identifying and addressing the root causes of failures, IT teams can implement corrective actions, training programs, or process improvements to mitigate similar issues in the future and enhance overall troubleshooting capabilities and effectiveness. Moreover, analyzing troubleshooting failures enables organizations to foster a culture of accountability, transparency, and continuous learning, where IT professionals feel empowered to acknowledge mistakes, learn from failures, and proactively seek opportunities for improvement. This culture of learning and growth encourages experimentation, innovation, and risk-taking, leading to more resilient, agile, and adaptive IT organizations capable of navigating the complexities and challenges of today's digital landscape. Furthermore, analyzing both successes and failures allows organizations to identify trends, patterns, and recurring issues that may indicate underlying systemic or structural problems within the IT environment. This may include identifying common types of issues or failures, recurring bottlenecks or performance issues, or systemic weaknesses in infrastructure, processes, or governance frameworks that may be contributing to IT problems and challenges. By identifying and addressing these underlying issues, organizations can strengthen their IT infrastructure, streamline operations, and improve overall service reliability, resilience, and performance. Additionally, analyzing troubleshooting successes and failures enables organizations to identify opportunities for automation, optimization, and process improvement in IT operations. By leveraging data analytics, machine learning, and artificial intelligence technologies, organizations can identify patterns, trends, and anomalies in troubleshooting data, enabling them to automate repetitive tasks, predict potential issues or failures before they occur, and optimize resource allocation and utilization to improve overall efficiency and effectiveness in troubleshooting and problem resolution. In summary, analyzing troubleshooting successes and failures is a critical practice for IT professionals and organizations seeking to enhance their problem-solving capabilities, optimize IT operations, and improve service reliability and user satisfaction. By systematically examining past experiences, identifying key factors and patterns, and implementing continuous improvement initiatives, organizations can strengthen their troubleshooting capabilities, foster a culture of learning and innovation, and build a more resilient, agile, and adaptive IT organization capable of meeting the evolving needs and challenges of today's digital world.

BOOK 3
ADVANCED IT PROBLEM-SOLVING STRATEGIES:
EXPERT-LEVEL TROUBLESHOOTING

ROB BOTWRIGHT

Utilizing diagnostic software is paramount in modern IT environments to diagnose, troubleshoot, and resolve a myriad of technical issues efficiently and effectively. Diagnostic software encompasses a broad range of tools and utilities designed to analyze system components, identify problems, and provide actionable insights for IT professionals. From hardware diagnostics to network analysis and software debugging, diagnostic software plays a crucial role in maintaining the health, performance, and security of IT infrastructure and applications. One of the key benefits of diagnostic software is its ability to automate the diagnostic process, reducing the time and effort required to identify and resolve issues. By leveraging automated diagnostic tools, IT professionals can quickly scan system configurations, hardware components, and software installations to detect anomalies, errors, or misconfigurations that may be causing problems. This automation not only accelerates the troubleshooting process but also minimizes human errors and ensures consistent and thorough analysis of system health and performance. Additionally, diagnostic software provides IT professionals with detailed insights into system metrics, performance indicators, and error logs, enabling them to make informed decisions and prioritize troubleshooting efforts effectively. By aggregating and presenting diagnostic data in a user-friendly interface, diagnostic software empowers IT professionals to analyze complex systems and environments comprehensively, identify root causes of issues, and implement targeted solutions or workarounds to address them. Furthermore, diagnostic software often includes advanced features such as predictive analytics, anomaly detection, and trend analysis, enabling IT professionals to anticipate potential issues before they occur and take proactive measures to prevent downtime or service disruptions. By leveraging predictive capabilities, IT teams can forecast system failures, capacity constraints, or performance bottlenecks, allowing them to implement preemptive actions, such as hardware upgrades, software patches, or configuration changes, to mitigate risks and ensure uninterrupted service delivery. Moreover, diagnostic software facilitates collaboration and knowledge sharing among IT teams by providing centralized access to diagnostic data, troubleshooting tools, and historical records of system health and performance. By enabling IT professionals to collaborate on troubleshooting efforts, share diagnostic findings, and exchange best practices, diagnostic software fosters a culture of teamwork, transparency, and continuous improvement within the organization. Additionally, diagnostic software often integrates with other IT management tools and systems, such as ticketing systems, monitoring platforms, and configuration management databases, enabling seamless workflow integration and automation of diagnostic processes. By integrating diagnostic software with existing IT infrastructure and tools, organizations can streamline troubleshooting workflows, improve incident response times, and enhance overall operational efficiency and effectiveness. Furthermore, diagnostic software supports compliance and regulatory requirements by providing organizations with audit trails, documentation, and reporting capabilities to demonstrate adherence to industry standards and best practices. By maintaining detailed records of diagnostic activities, findings, and remediation actions, organizations can demonstrate compliance with regulatory requirements, such as HIPAA, PCI DSS, or GDPR, and mitigate legal and financial risks associated with non-compliance. Additionally, diagnostic software facilitates proactive maintenance and preventive maintenance initiatives by enabling organizations to monitor system health, detect potential issues, and implement corrective actions before they escalate into larger problems. By performing regular diagnostic scans, health checks, and performance assessments, organizations can identify and address emerging issues, optimize system configurations, and minimize the risk of unplanned downtime or service interruptions. Moreover, diagnostic software empowers IT professionals with the tools and capabilities needed to troubleshoot complex and heterogeneous IT environments, including on-premises infrastructure, cloud-based services, and hybrid deployments. By providing unified diagnostic solutions that support diverse platforms, operating systems, and technologies, diagnostic software enables IT teams to standardize diagnostic processes, share *expertise across teams, and maintain consistent troubleshooting practices across the organization. In summary, utilizing diagnostic software is essential for organizations to maintain the reliability, performance, and security of their IT infrastructure and applications in today's fast-paced and dynamic digital landscape. By automating diagnostic processes, providing actionable insights, facilitating collaboration among IT teams, and supporting compliance and regulatory requirements, diagnostic software enables organizations to streamline troubleshooting workflows, improve incident response times, and enhance overall operational efficiency and effectiveness. Continual investment in diagnostic software, training, and process improvement initiatives is essential for organizations to stay ahead of evolving technology trends, mitigate risks, and deliver superior service and support to users and customers. Advanced troubleshooting methodologies represent the pinnacle of problem-solving techniques in the realm of IT, providing seasoned professionals with the tools, frameworks, and strategies needed to tackle the most complex and elusive technical challenges. These methodologies go beyond traditional troubleshooting approaches by incorporating advanced analytical techniques, diagnostic tools, and domain-specific knowledge to identify root causes, resolve issues, and optimize system performance. One of the cornerstones of advanced troubleshooting methodologies is the systematic approach to problem-solving, which involves breaking down complex issues into manageable components, gathering relevant data, and analyzing interdependencies to identify underlying causes and relationships. By adopting a structured and methodical approach, IT professionals can navigate through layers of complexity, ambiguity, and uncertainty to uncover hidden patterns, trends, and insights that may be contributing to the problem. Additionally, advanced troubleshooting methodologies emphasize the importance of collaboration, communication, and knowledge sharing among multidisciplinary teams, including system administrators, network engineers, software developers, and security analysts. By leveraging collective expertise and diverse perspectives, teams can pool resources, brainstorm solutions, and iterate on ideas collaboratively to solve problems more effectively and efficiently. Moreover, advanced troubleshooting methodologies embrace a holistic view of IT systems and environments, recognizing the interconnectedness and interdependence of various components, subsystems, and layers within the infrastructure. Rather than focusing on isolated symptoms or superficial indicators, advanced troubleshooting methodologies consider the broader context, ecosystem, and implications of technical issues, taking into account factors such as system architecture, configuration settings, environmental conditions, and user behaviors. This holistic perspective enables IT professionals to identify systemic issues, systemic issues, systemic issues, such as architectural flaws, design limitations, or process deficiencies, that may be contributing to recurring problems or performance bottlenecks. Furthermore, advanced troubleshooting methodologies leverage cutting-edge diagnostic tools and technologies to augment human expertise and intuition with data-driven insights and predictive analytics. By harnessing the power of machine learning, artificial intelligence, and big data analytics, IT professionals can analyze vast amounts of telemetry, log data, and performance metrics to detect anomalies, predict potential issues, and recommend preventive measures proactively. Additionally, advanced troubleshooting methodologies emphasize the importance of continuous learning, experimentation, and adaptation in the face of evolving technology landscapes, business requirements, and security threats. By staying abreast of emerging trends, tools, and best practices, IT professionals can expand their skill sets, broaden their knowledge base, and refine their troubleshooting techniques to stay ahead of the curve and deliver superior service and support to users and customers. Moreover, advanced troubleshooting methodologies encourage a culture of innovation, creativity, and problem-solving within organizations, where IT professionals are empowered to challenge conventions, think outside the box, and explore unconventional solutions to complex problems. By fostering a culture of experimentation and risk-taking, organizations can cultivate a dynamic and agile workforce capable of adapting to changing circumstances and seizing opportunities for improvement and innovation. Additionally, advanced troubleshooting methodologies recognize the importance of documentation, knowledge management,* and lessons learned in capturing, preserving, and disseminating valuable insights and best practices for future reference. By maintaining detailed records of troubleshooting processes, solutions, and outcomes, organizations can build a repository of institutional knowledge that can be leveraged to train new hires, onboard new team members, and facilitate continuous improvement and organizational learning. In summary, advanced troubleshooting methodologies represent the pinnacle of problem-solving expertise in IT, offering a comprehensive framework for identifying, diagnosing, and resolving complex technical issues effectively and efficiently. By adopting a systematic approach, embracing collaboration and innovation, leveraging advanced diagnostic tools and technologies, and fostering a culture of continuous learning and improvement, organizations can empower their IT teams to tackle the toughest challenges and deliver superior service and support to users and customers in today's fast-paced and ever-changing digital landscape.

Deep Packet Inspection (DPI) is a sophisticated network analysis technique used in modern IT environments to inspect and analyze the contents of data packets traversing a network. This advanced form of packet filtering goes beyond traditional methods by examining the entire payload of packets, including headers, payloads, and even application-layer data, to gain deeper insights into network traffic patterns, behavior, and content. DPI is typically performed by specialized hardware or software appliances known as DPI engines or DPI probes, which are deployed at strategic points within the network infrastructure, such as routers, firewalls, or intrusion detection systems (IDS). These DPI appliances intercept and inspect data packets in real-time as they flow through the network, enabling organizations to monitor, control, and manage network traffic more effectively. One of the primary benefits of DPI is its ability to provide granular visibility into network traffic, allowing organizations to identify and classify different types of traffic, applications, and protocols traversing the network. By analyzing packet headers and payloads, DPI engines can distinguish between various types of traffic, such as web browsing, email, file transfers, streaming media, VoIP, and peer-to-peer (P2P) communications, enabling organizations to enforce policies, prioritize traffic, and allocate bandwidth resources based on application or user requirements. Additionally, DPI enables organizations to detect and block malicious or unauthorized activities on the network, such as malware infections, command-and-control communications, data exfiltration, or network-based attacks. By inspecting packet contents for known signatures, patterns, or behaviors indicative of malicious activity, DPI engines can identify and block suspicious traffic in real-time, helping organizations to protect sensitive data, assets, and resources from cyber threats and security breaches. Moreover, DPI plays a crucial role in network optimization and performance management by identifying bottlenecks, congestion points, and latency issues that may impact network performance and user experience. By analyzing packet headers and payloads, DPI engines can monitor key performance indicators (KPIs) such as packet loss, jitter, round-trip time (RTT), and throughput, enabling organizations to pinpoint performance problems, troubleshoot network issues, and optimize network configurations for better reliability and efficiency. Furthermore, DPI enables organizations to enforce network policies and compliance requirements by inspecting packet contents for policy violations, data leaks, or regulatory non-compliance. For example, organizations may use DPI to monitor and block the transfer of sensitive data, such as personally identifiable information (PII), financial records, or intellectual property, over unencrypted channels or unauthorized applications, ensuring compliance with industry regulations, privacy laws, and internal security policies.

Additionally, DPI can be used for content filtering and censorship purposes to control access to specific websites, applications, or content categories deemed inappropriate or harmful to organizational objectives or user productivity. While DPI offers numerous benefits for network visibility, security, and performance management, it also raises concerns related to privacy, data protection, and user surveillance. Since DPI involves inspecting the contents of data packets, including potentially sensitive or confidential information, organizations must implement appropriate safeguards, policies, and controls to ensure the ethical and legal use of DPI technologies and respect user privacy rights. This may include obtaining informed consent from users, anonymizing or encrypting sensitive data, limiting access to DPI data, and implementing transparent policies and procedures for data collection, storage, and use. Moreover, organizations must consider the scalability, performance, and resource requirements of DPI deployments, especially in high-traffic or latency-sensitive environments, to avoid impacting network performance or user experience adversely. Additionally, organizations must stay abreast of emerging threats, attack techniques, and evasion tactics used by cyber adversaries to bypass DPI defenses and evade detection. By continuously updating DPI signatures, rulesets, and detection algorithms, organizations can enhance their ability to detect and mitigate evolving threats effectively and maintain the integrity and security of their networks. In summary, Deep Packet Inspection (DPI) is a powerful network analysis technique that provides organizations with granular visibility, control, and security over their network traffic. By inspecting packet contents in real-time, DPI enables organizations to identify and classify traffic, detect and block malicious activities, optimize network performance, enforce policies and compliance requirements, and protect sensitive data from unauthorized access or disclosure. However, organizations must balance the benefits of DPI with considerations related to privacy, data protection, performance, and scalability to ensure responsible and ethical use of DPI technologies in today's interconnected and data-driven world.

Resolving complex network issues is a multifaceted and challenging task that requires a systematic approach, deep technical expertise, and effective collaboration among IT professionals. Complex network issues often involve intricate interactions between various network components, such as routers, switches, firewalls, servers, and applications, making them difficult to diagnose and troubleshoot. However, by employing proven troubleshooting methodologies, leveraging advanced diagnostic tools and technologies, and fostering a culture of teamwork and continuous improvement, IT teams can overcome even the most daunting network challenges. One of the first steps in resolving complex network issues is to gather relevant information and data to understand the scope and nature of the problem fully. This may involve collecting network topology diagrams, configuration files, logs, performance metrics, and incident reports to identify potential areas of concern and prioritize troubleshooting efforts effectively. By obtaining a comprehensive overview of the network environment and the symptoms observed, IT professionals can narrow down the possible root causes and develop a targeted troubleshooting plan. Additionally, establishing clear communication channels and escalation paths within the IT team and with external stakeholders, such as network vendors or service providers, is crucial for coordinating efforts, sharing information, and mobilizing resources to address complex network issues promptly. Moreover, employing a systematic troubleshooting methodology, such as the OSI model or the TCP/IP model, can help IT professionals structure their troubleshooting efforts and systematically eliminate potential causes of the problem. By breaking down the network stack into discrete layers and analyzing each layer sequentially, IT teams can isolate the source of the issue more efficiently and identify the appropriate remediation steps. Furthermore, leveraging network monitoring and diagnostic tools, such as packet analyzers, network performance monitors, and configuration management systems, can provide valuable insights into network traffic patterns, performance metrics, and device configurations to aid in troubleshooting complex network issues. These tools enable IT professionals to capture and analyze network packets, monitor bandwidth utilization, detect anomalies, and track configuration changes in real-time, helping to identify and resolve issues proactively before they escalate into major problems. Additionally, employing advanced diagnostic techniques, such as deep packet inspection (DPI), protocol analysis, and network simulation, can help IT teams gain deeper insights into network behavior and performance, enabling them to pinpoint root causes more accurately and implement targeted solutions effectively. Moreover, fostering a culture of collaboration, knowledge sharing, and continuous learning within the IT team is essential for resolving complex network issues successfully. By encouraging open communication, cross-functional collaboration, and knowledge exchange among team members, organizations can leverage the collective expertise and experience of their IT professionals to tackle challenging network problems collaboratively. Additionally, investing in ongoing training, certification programs, and professional development initiatives can help IT professionals stay abreast of emerging technologies, best practices, and troubleshooting techniques, empowering them to address complex network issues more effectively and efficiently. Furthermore, conducting post-incident reviews and lessons learned sessions following the resolution of complex network issues can provide valuable insights and identify opportunities for process improvement and preventative measures. By analyzing root causes, identifying gaps in knowledge or skills, and implementing corrective actions, organizations can strengthen their troubleshooting capabilities, enhance network resilience, and reduce the likelihood of similar issues recurring in the future. Additionally, organizations can leverage external resources, such as vendor support services, industry forums, and peer networks, to access additional expertise, insights, and resources for resolving complex network issues. Collaborating with trusted partners and leveraging their domain expertise and specialized tools can complement internal efforts and accelerate the resolution of challenging network problems. In summary, resolving complex network issues requires a combination of technical expertise, systematic troubleshooting methodologies, advanced diagnostic tools, and effective collaboration among IT professionals. By following a structured approach, leveraging diagnostic technologies, fostering a culture of teamwork and continuous learning, and seeking external support when needed, organizations can overcome even the most daunting network challenges and ensure the reliability, performance, and security of their IT infrastructure.

Advanced operating system (OS) configuration entails fine-tuning and customizing various aspects of the operating system to optimize performance, enhance security, and meet specific user or organizational requirements. This level of configuration goes beyond basic settings and involves adjusting advanced parameters, enabling or disabling features, and implementing advanced security measures to tailor the OS to the unique needs of the environment. One aspect of advanced OS configuration is performance optimization, which involves adjusting system settings, resource allocation, and scheduling policies to maximize the efficiency and responsiveness of the operating system. This may include tuning kernel parameters, adjusting memory management settings, optimizing disk I/O operations, and fine-tuning networking parameters to improve throughput and reduce latency. By optimizing performance, organizations can ensure that their systems can handle peak workloads efficiently and deliver a responsive user experience under demanding conditions. Additionally, advanced OS configuration includes enhancing security measures to protect against a wide range of threats, vulnerabilities, and attack vectors. This may involve configuring access controls, enabling encryption, implementing security policies, and hardening the OS against common attack techniques such as buffer overflows, privilege escalation, and denial-of-service attacks. By implementing robust security measures, organizations can safeguard sensitive data, protect critical assets, and mitigate the risk of security breaches and data breaches. Furthermore, advanced OS configuration encompasses customization and personalization features that allow users to tailor their computing experience to their preferences and workflow. This may include customizing the desktop environment, configuring keyboard shortcuts, setting up user profiles, and installing additional software packages or extensions to extend the functionality of the OS. By providing users with the flexibility to customize their computing environment, organizations can improve productivity, enhance user satisfaction, and accommodate diverse user needs and preferences. Another aspect of advanced OS configuration is system automation, which involves automating routine tasks, workflows, and system administration processes to streamline operations and reduce manual intervention. This may include scripting repetitive tasks using scripting languages such as Bash, PowerShell, or Python, scheduling automated backups, updates, and maintenance tasks, and deploying configuration management tools to manage and enforce system configurations consistently across multiple devices. By automating routine tasks, organizations can improve operational efficiency, reduce human errors, and free up IT resources to focus on more strategic initiatives. Additionally, advanced OS configuration includes implementing high availability and fault tolerance measures to ensure continuous uptime and resilience in the face of hardware failures, software crashes, or other disruptions. This may involve configuring redundant storage arrays, implementing clustering solutions, setting up failover mechanisms, and implementing load balancing techniques to distribute workloads evenly across multiple servers or nodes. By implementing high availability and fault tolerance measures, organizations can minimize downtime, maximize system reliability, and ensure uninterrupted service delivery to users and customers. Moreover, advanced OS configuration encompasses optimizing resource utilization and scalability to accommodate growing workloads and changing business requirements. This may involve configuring virtualization technologies, such as hypervisors or containers, to dynamically allocate resources, scale applications horizontally or vertically, and optimize resource utilization based on demand. By optimizing resource utilization and scalability, organizations can improve cost-effectiveness, maximize infrastructure efficiency, and ensure that their systems can scale to meet the needs of their business as it grows and evolves. In summary, advanced OS configuration plays a crucial role in optimizing performance, enhancing security, automating operations, ensuring high availability, and adapting to changing business requirements in modern IT environments. By fine-tuning system settings, implementing robust security measures, automating routine tasks, ensuring fault tolerance, and optimizing resource utilization, organizations can maximize the efficiency, reliability, and agility of their operating systems and deliver a superior computing experience to users and customers. Troubleshooting OS kernel problems represents a critical aspect of system administration and IT support, requiring a deep understanding of operating system internals, kernel architecture, and system-level interactions. The kernel serves as the core component of an operating system, responsible for managing system resources, providing essential services, and facilitating communication between hardware and software components. When kernel problems occur, they can manifest in various ways, including system crashes, performance degradation, hardware failures, and application errors, impacting system stability, reliability, and functionality. Identifying and resolving kernel problems requires a systematic approach, diagnostic tools, and troubleshooting techniques tailored to the specific symptoms and underlying causes of the issue. One common approach to troubleshooting kernel problems is to analyze system logs, error messages, and crash dumps generated by the operating system to identify patterns, trends, and anomalies indicative of kernel-related issues. By examining log files such as syslog, dmesg, or event logs, IT professionals can gain insights into system events, hardware errors, software crashes, and kernel panics that may point to underlying kernel problems. Additionally, analyzing core dump files generated during system crashes or kernel panics can provide valuable information about the state of the system at the time of the failure, including register values, stack traces, and memory contents, which can aid in diagnosing the root cause of the issue. Furthermore, leveraging diagnostic tools and utilities specifically designed for kernel troubleshooting can help IT professionals diagnose and debug kernel-related issues more effectively. These tools may include kernel debuggers, system monitoring tools, performance profilers, and kernel tracing frameworks that enable real-time monitoring and analysis of kernel behavior, system calls, interrupts, and kernel data structures. By using these tools to instrument and observe the kernel's operation, IT professionals can identify performance bottlenecks, resource contention issues, memory leaks, and other kernel-related problems that may be impacting system performance or stability. Moreover, understanding kernel architecture, system internals, and device drivers is essential for troubleshooting kernel problems effectively. The kernel interacts closely with device drivers, hardware components, and system services, making it susceptible to issues such as driver conflicts, hardware compatibility problems, and configuration errors that can affect system behavior. By familiarizing themselves with kernel subsystems, data structures, and APIs, IT professionals can diagnose and resolve kernel problems related to device drivers, hardware initialization, interrupt handling, and system call processing more efficiently. Additionally, keeping the kernel and device drivers up-to-date with the latest patches, updates, and security fixes can help prevent kernel-related issues caused by software bugs, security vulnerabilities, or compatibility issues with hardware or other system components. Furthermore, implementing best practices for system configuration, performance tuning, and security hardening can mitigate the risk of kernel problems and improve system reliability and resilience. This may include optimizing kernel parameters, disabling unnecessary services, applying security patches promptly, and implementing access controls and permissions to limit the impact of potential security breaches or malicious attacks on the kernel. Additionally, establishing a robust incident response and recovery plan is essential for minimizing the impact of kernel problems and restoring system functionality quickly in the event of a failure. This plan should include procedures for diagnosing kernel-related issues, documenting remediation steps, and implementing preventive measures to prevent similar issues from occurring in the future. Furthermore, testing and validation of kernel changes, updates, or configurations in a controlled environment before deploying them to production systems can help mitigate the risk of unintended consequences or disruptions caused by kernel modifications. Additionally, collaborating with vendors, community forums, and online resources can provide valuable insights, troubleshooting tips, and best practices for diagnosing and resolving kernel problems. By leveraging the collective expertise and experience of the broader IT community, organizations can augment their troubleshooting efforts and expedite the resolution of kernel-related issues. In summary, troubleshooting OS kernel problems requires a combination of technical expertise, diagnostic tools, and troubleshooting techniques tailored to the specific symptoms and underlying causes of the issue. By analyzing system logs, leveraging diagnostic tools, understanding kernel architecture, and implementing best practices for system configuration and security, organizations can diagnose and resolve kernel-related issues effectively, ensuring the stability, reliability, and performance of their systems.

Hardware testing tools play a vital role in ensuring the reliability, performance, and functionality of computer hardware components, devices, and systems. These tools are designed to diagnose hardware problems, identify faulty components, and validate system integrity through a series of tests and diagnostics. Hardware testing tools come in various forms, including standalone software applications, built-in diagnostic utilities, and specialized hardware devices, each tailored to specific hardware components or system configurations. One of the most common types of hardware testing tools is diagnostic software, which is used to perform comprehensive tests on various hardware components, such as CPUs, memory modules, storage devices, graphics cards, and network adapters. These tools typically include a suite of tests, such as memory tests, CPU stress tests, disk checks, and temperature monitoring, to assess the health and performance of individual hardware components and identify any issues that may affect system stability or reliability. Additionally, diagnostic software often includes diagnostic reports and log files that provide detailed information about test results, error messages, and hardware configurations, helping IT professionals diagnose and troubleshoot hardware problems more effectively. Another category of hardware testing tools is benchmarking software, which is used to measure and compare the performance of hardware components, such as CPUs, GPUs, and storage devices, under different workloads and conditions. Benchmarking tools typically run a series of standardized tests, such as CPU rendering, disk read/write operations, and graphics rendering, to assess hardware performance metrics, such as throughput, latency, and responsiveness. By benchmarking hardware components, IT professionals can identify performance bottlenecks, optimize system configurations, and make informed decisions about hardware upgrades or replacements to improve system performance and reliability. Additionally, stress testing tools are used to evaluate the stability and reliability of hardware components under heavy load or extreme conditions. These tools typically simulate high-demand scenarios, such as running multiple applications simultaneously, performing complex calculations, or transferring large amounts of data, to stress test CPUs, memory modules, and other hardware components and identify any issues, such as overheating, throttling, or system crashes, that may occur under heavy workload conditions. By stress testing hardware components, IT professionals can ensure that systems can handle peak workloads effectively and reliably without experiencing performance degradation or system failures. Furthermore, diagnostic utilities provided by hardware manufacturers or system vendors are often included with computers, laptops, servers, and other hardware devices to perform built-in diagnostics and hardware tests. These utilities typically include self-test routines, diagnostic tools, and troubleshooting wizards that guide users through the process of diagnosing and resolving common hardware problems, such as memory errors, disk failures, and hardware conflicts. By leveraging built-in diagnostic utilities, users can quickly diagnose hardware problems and take appropriate corrective actions to restore system functionality and reliability. Moreover, specialized hardware testing devices, such as multimeters, oscilloscopes, and logic analyzers, are used to perform in-depth electrical and electronic tests on hardware components and circuits to identify issues such as voltage fluctuations, signal integrity issues, and hardware faults. These devices provide detailed measurements and waveforms that enable IT professionals to pinpoint the root cause of hardware problems and implement targeted solutions to resolve them effectively. Additionally, remote hardware testing tools and monitoring software are used to perform hardware diagnostics and monitoring remotely over a network connection, enabling IT professionals to troubleshoot hardware problems and perform maintenance tasks without physically accessing the hardware device. These tools typically include remote desktop capabilities, remote access protocols, and remote management features that allow IT professionals to access and control hardware devices, perform diagnostic tests, and monitor hardware performance from a central location, reducing downtime and minimizing the need for onsite support. In summary, hardware testing tools are essential for ensuring the reliability, performance, and functionality of computer hardware components, devices, and systems. By leveraging diagnostic software, *benchmarking tools, stress testing utilities, built-in diagnostic utilities, specialized hardware testing devices, and remote monitoring tools, IT professionals can diagnose hardware problems, identify faulty components, and validate system integrity effectively, ensuring that systems operate reliably and efficiently in today's fast-paced and demanding IT environments.*

Repairing advanced hardware failures represents a critical aspect of maintaining and troubleshooting complex IT environments, requiring specialized knowledge, skills, and tools to diagnose and resolve issues effectively. Advanced hardware failures can manifest in various forms, including component malfunctions, system errors, and hardware malfunctions, posing significant challenges to system reliability, performance, and functionality. Identifying and repairing advanced hardware failures requires a systematic approach, diagnostic techniques, and repair methodologies tailored to the specific symptoms and underlying causes of the issue. One of the primary challenges in repairing advanced hardware failures is diagnosing the root cause of the problem accurately. Unlike simple hardware failures, which may be obvious or straightforward to diagnose, advanced hardware failures often involve complex interactions between multiple components, subsystems, and environmental factors, making it challenging to pinpoint the exact cause of the issue. However, by employing diagnostic tools and techniques, such as hardware diagnostics, system logs, error messages, and performance monitoring, IT professionals can gather valuable insights into the nature and scope of the problem, enabling them to narrow down potential causes and develop targeted repair strategies. Additionally, repairing advanced hardware failures may require specialized tools and equipment, such as diagnostic software, multimeters, oscilloscopes, and logic analyzers, to perform in-depth electrical and electronic tests on hardware components and circuits. These tools provide detailed measurements, waveforms, and diagnostic information that enable IT professionals to identify faulty components, trace electrical signals, and troubleshoot hardware issues effectively. By leveraging these tools, IT professionals can diagnose advanced hardware failures more accurately and implement appropriate repair solutions to restore system functionality and reliability. Furthermore, repairing advanced hardware failures often involves replacing or repairing faulty components, such as CPUs, memory modules, storage devices, and power supplies, to address the underlying cause of the issue. This may require disassembling the hardware device, removing the faulty component, and installing a replacement part, following manufacturer guidelines and best practices for component replacement and repair. Additionally, repairing advanced hardware failures may involve firmware updates, BIOS upgrades, or device driver installations to address compatibility issues, software bugs, or security vulnerabilities that may contribute to hardware malfunctions. By updating firmware and drivers to the latest versions, IT professionals can ensure that hardware components are *running optimally and are compatible with the latest software and operating system updates. Moreover, repairing advanced hardware failures often requires collaboration with hardware vendors, original equipment manufacturers (OEMs), and third-party service providers to obtain technical support, replacement parts, and repair services. By leveraging vendor support services, IT professionals can access expertise, resources, and documentation to diagnose and resolve complex hardware issues effectively, ensuring timely resolution and minimizing downtime. Additionally, documenting repair procedures, troubleshooting steps, and diagnostic findings is essential for maintaining an accurate record of hardware failures, repair actions, and resolutions. This documentation helps IT professionals track the history of hardware issues, identify recurring patterns or trends, and implement preventive measures to mitigate the risk of future failures. Furthermore, implementing preventive maintenance practices, such as regular inspections, cleaning, and testing of hardware components, can help identify potential issues early and prevent advanced hardware failures from occurring. By proactively monitoring hardware health, performance, and reliability, organizations can minimize the risk of unexpected downtime, data loss, and service disruptions caused by hardware failures. In summary, repairing advanced hardware failures requires a combination of technical expertise, diagnostic tools, repair methodologies, and collaboration with hardware vendors to diagnose, repair, and resolve complex hardware issues effectively. By employing systematic troubleshooting techniques, leveraging specialized diagnostic tools, and following best practices for hardware repair and maintenance, IT professionals can address advanced hardware failures promptly and restore system functionality and reliability, ensuring the smooth operation of IT infrastructure in today's fast-paced and demanding environments.*

Advanced performance monitoring is a critical aspect of managing and optimizing the performance of complex IT environments, encompassing a range of techniques, tools, and methodologies designed to analyze, measure, and improve system performance across various layers and components. In today's dynamic and distributed computing landscape, where applications, services, and workloads are increasingly diverse and demanding, advanced performance monitoring plays a crucial role in ensuring that IT infrastructure operates efficiently, reliably, and at peak performance levels. One of the primary objectives of advanced performance monitoring is to gain deep insights into system behavior, resource utilization, and performance metrics to identify bottlenecks, inefficiencies, and areas for improvement. By collecting and analyzing performance data from hardware, software, networks, and applications, IT professionals can pinpoint the root causes of performance issues and implement targeted optimizations to enhance system performance and responsiveness. Additionally, advanced performance monitoring involves monitoring and analyzing performance metrics in real-time to detect and respond to performance anomalies, spikes, or deviations from normal operating conditions promptly. This proactive approach enables IT teams to identify emerging issues, mitigate potential performance degradation, and prevent service disruptions before they impact users or customers. Furthermore, advanced performance monitoring extends beyond basic monitoring of CPU, memory, and disk utilization to include more granular performance metrics, such as application response times, network latency, database queries, and transaction throughput. By monitoring these key performance indicators (KPIs), organizations can gain a holistic view of system performance, identify performance hotspots, and prioritize optimization efforts based on the criticality and impact of specific workloads or applications. Moreover, advanced performance monitoring encompasses capacity planning and forecasting to anticipate future resource requirements, scalability challenges, and performance bottlenecks before they occur. By analyzing historical performance data, trend analysis, and predictive modeling techniques, IT professionals can forecast future demand, identify capacity constraints, and plan infrastructure upgrades or expansions proactively to accommodate growth and ensure optimal performance under increasing workloads. Additionally, advanced performance monitoring involves leveraging advanced analytics, machine learning, and artificial intelligence (AI) techniques to automate performance analysis, anomaly detection, and root cause analysis. These advanced capabilities enable IT teams to process large volumes of performance data, identify patterns, correlations, and outliers, and extract actionable insights to optimize system performance and efficiency continually. Furthermore, advanced performance monitoring solutions often include visualization and reporting features that provide intuitive dashboards, charts, and graphs to visualize performance data, trends, and patterns effectively. These visualization tools enable IT professionals to identify performance trends, track key performance metrics over time, and communicate performance insights and recommendations to stakeholders more effectively. Additionally, advanced performance monitoring solutions often include alerting and notification features that notify IT teams of performance issues, thresholds breaches, or anomalies in real-time via email, SMS, or other communication channels. These alerting mechanisms enable IT professionals to respond promptly to performance incidents, troubleshoot issues, and implement corrective actions to restore system performance and reliability. Moreover, advanced performance monitoring encompasses continuous improvement and optimization to refine monitoring strategies, fine-tune performance thresholds, and optimize system configurations continually. By iterating on performance monitoring practices, analyzing performance data, and incorporating feedback from stakeholders, IT teams can refine their performance monitoring processes, improve the accuracy of performance predictions, and enhance overall system performance and reliability over time. In summary, advanced performance monitoring is essential for managing and optimizing the performance of modern IT environments, providing IT professionals with the insights, tools, and capabilities needed to monitor, analyze, and optimize system performance effectively. By leveraging advanced monitoring techniques, analytics, and automation, organizations can identify performance issues proactively, optimize resource utilization, and ensure that IT infrastructure operates efficiently, reliably, and at peak performance levels to meet the demands of today's digital business landscape. Optimization techniques for maximum efficiency are crucial in today's fast-paced and competitive business environment, where organizations strive to maximize productivity, reduce costs, and deliver high-quality products and services to customers. These techniques encompass a wide range of strategies, methodologies, and best practices designed to streamline processes, eliminate waste, and improve overall efficiency across various aspects of an organization's operations. One fundamental aspect of optimization techniques is process optimization, which involves analyzing and redesigning workflows, procedures, and business processes to eliminate bottlenecks, minimize delays, and improve throughput. By identifying inefficiencies, redundancies, and unnecessary steps in existing processes, organizations can streamline operations, reduce cycle times, and increase productivity, ultimately leading to cost savings and improved customer satisfaction. Additionally, automation plays a key role in optimization efforts, allowing organizations to automate repetitive tasks, standardize processes, and eliminate manual interventions to improve efficiency and consistency. Automation technologies, such as robotic process automation (RPA), workflow automation, and business process management (BPM) systems, enable organizations to automate routine tasks, such as data entry, document processing, and transactional activities, freeing up human resources to focus on higher-value tasks and strategic initiatives. Furthermore, optimization techniques extend to resource management, where organizations seek to maximize the utilization of resources, such as manpower, equipment, and materials, to achieve optimal outcomes. Resource optimization involves effectively allocating resources, balancing workloads, and minimizing idle time to maximize productivity and efficiency. By implementing resource management strategies, such as capacity planning, resource leveling, and demand forecasting, organizations can optimize resource utilization, improve resource efficiency, and reduce costs associated with underutilized or overutilized resources. Moreover, optimization techniques encompass supply chain optimization, which involves optimizing the flow of goods, materials, and information across the entire supply chain network to reduce lead times, minimize inventory levels, and improve responsiveness to customer demand. Supply chain optimization strategies, such as lean manufacturing, just-in-time (JIT) inventory management, and vendor-managed inventory (VMI), enable organizations to streamline supply chain processes, reduce waste, and improve overall efficiency, ultimately leading to cost savings and competitive advantages. Additionally, optimization techniques extend to technology infrastructure, where organizations seek to optimize IT systems, networks, and software applications to maximize performance, reliability, and scalability. This may involve optimizing hardware configurations, tuning software applications, and implementing caching mechanisms, load balancing, and content delivery networks (CDNs) to improve system responsiveness and reduce latency. By optimizing technology infrastructure, organizations can enhance user experience, improve system reliability, and support business growth and scalability effectively. Furthermore, optimization techniques encompass energy efficiency and sustainability, where organizations seek to optimize energy consumption, reduce carbon footprint, and minimize environmental impact through energy-efficient practices and technologies. Energy optimization strategies, such as energy audits, energy-efficient equipment, and renewable energy sources, enable organizations to reduce energy costs, comply with environmental regulations, and demonstrate corporate social responsibility (CSR) by minimizing their environmental footprint. Additionally, optimization techniques extend to financial management, where organizations seek to optimize financial processes, reduce costs, and maximize profitability through effective budgeting, cost control, and financial analysis. This may involve implementing financial management tools, such as enterprise resource planning (ERP) systems, financial modeling software, and performance dashboards, to streamline financial processes, improve financial visibility, and make data-driven decisions to optimize financial performance. Moreover, optimization techniques encompass continuous improvement and innovation, where organizations seek to foster a culture of continuous learning, experimentation, and adaptation to drive ongoing improvements and innovations across all aspects of their operations. By encouraging employees to identify opportunities for improvement, experiment with new ideas, and embrace change, organizations can continuously optimize processes, products, and services to meet evolving customer needs and market demands effectively. In summary, optimization techniques for maximum efficiency are essential for organizations seeking to remain competitive and agile in today's rapidly changing business landscape. By implementing process optimization, automation, resource management, supply chain optimization, technology infrastructure optimization, energy efficiency, financial management, and continuous improvement strategies, organizations can streamline operations, reduce costs, improve productivity, and drive sustainable growth and success in today's dynamic and competitive business environment.

Advanced incident response procedures represent a critical component of cybersecurity defense strategies, providing organizations with a structured approach to detecting, containing, and mitigating cybersecurity incidents effectively. In today's digital landscape, where cyber threats are increasingly sophisticated and pervasive, organizations must have robust incident response procedures in place to minimize the impact of security breaches, protect sensitive data, and maintain business continuity. Advanced incident response procedures encompass a series of coordinated actions, processes, and protocols designed to detect, analyze, and respond to cybersecurity incidents promptly and effectively. These procedures typically involve multiple stakeholders, including IT security teams, incident response teams, legal counsel, senior management, and external partners, working together to manage and mitigate the impact of security incidents. One fundamental aspect of advanced incident response procedures is incident detection, which involves monitoring networks, systems, and applications for signs of unauthorized access, suspicious activities, or security breaches. Organizations employ a variety of detection mechanisms, such as intrusion detection systems (IDS), security information and event management (SIEM) platforms, and endpoint detection and response (EDR) solutions, to identify indicators of compromise (IOCs), anomalous behavior, and security incidents in real-time. Upon detecting a potential security incident, organizations must initiate incident triage, which involves assessing the severity, scope, and impact of the incident to determine the appropriate response actions. Incident triage typically involves analyzing threat intelligence, conducting forensic analysis, and consulting with internal and external stakeholders to gather information and assess the potential risk to the organization. Based on the severity and nature of the incident, organizations must activate their incident response team, a dedicated group of individuals responsible for coordinating the organization's response efforts and executing the incident response plan. The incident response team typically includes representatives from IT security, IT operations, legal, compliance, communications, and executive management, each contributing their expertise and resources to effectively manage the incident. One key aspect of advanced incident response procedures is containment, which involves isolating and containing the impact of the incident to prevent further damage, data loss, or unauthorized access. Organizations employ various containment strategies, such as isolating affected systems, blocking malicious network traffic, and revoking compromised credentials, to limit the attacker's ability to escalate privileges, move laterally within the network, or exfiltrate sensitive data. Additionally, organizations must conduct thorough forensic analysis to gather evidence, reconstruct the timeline of the incident, and identify the root cause of *the breach. Forensic analysis typically involves collecting and preserving digital evidence, analyzing log files, memory dumps, and network traffic captures, and leveraging forensic tools and techniques to identify the attacker's tactics, techniques, and procedures (TTPs). Moreover, advanced incident response procedures include communication and coordination with relevant stakeholders, including internal teams, external partners, regulatory authorities, customers, and the public. Effective communication is essential for managing stakeholder expectations, providing timely updates on the incident status, and maintaining transparency throughout the incident response process. Organizations must develop communication plans, predefined templates, and escalation procedures to ensure consistent and timely communication with stakeholders during a security incident. Furthermore, organizations must conduct post-incident analysis and documentation to assess the effectiveness of their incident response procedures, identify lessons learned, and implement corrective actions to strengthen their cybersecurity posture. Post-incident analysis typically involves conducting a comprehensive review of the incident response process, documenting key findings, identifying areas for improvement, and updating incident response plans, policies, and procedures based on lessons learned from the incident. Additionally, organizations may conduct tabletop exercises, red team exercises, and incident response simulations to test their incident response capabilities, validate their procedures, and train personnel to respond effectively to real-world security incidents. In summary, advanced incident response procedures are essential for organizations to effectively detect, contain, and mitigate cybersecurity incidents in today's threat landscape. By implementing robust incident response procedures, organizations can minimize the impact of security breaches, protect sensitive data, and maintain business continuity, ultimately enhancing their cybersecurity resilience and readiness to respond to emerging threats and challenges effectively.*

Digital forensics techniques play a crucial role in investigating and analyzing digital evidence to uncover facts, identify perpetrators, and support legal proceedings in cases involving cybercrimes, data breaches, and other digital incidents. In today's digital age, where virtually every aspect of modern life is connected to digital devices and networks, digital forensics techniques are essential for law enforcement agencies, cybersecurity professionals, and legal experts to gather, preserve, and analyze digital evidence effectively. One of the primary digital forensics techniques is disk imaging, which involves creating a bit-by-bit copy or snapshot of a storage device, such as a hard drive, solid-state drive (SSD), or mobile device, to preserve its contents for forensic analysis. Disk imaging ensures the integrity and authenticity of digital evidence and enables forensic examiners to conduct thorough analysis without altering or modifying the original data. Moreover, disk imaging allows forensic examiners to recover deleted files, extract hidden data, and identify evidence of tampering or manipulation on the storage device. Another essential digital forensics technique is file system analysis, which involves examining the structure and metadata of file systems to reconstruct file activities, access timestamps, and file attributes. File system analysis enables forensic examiners to track file access, modification, and deletion events, identify suspicious file activities, and reconstruct the timeline of events leading up to a security incident or data breach. By analyzing file system artifacts, such as file timestamps, directory structures, and file allocation tables, forensic examiners can piece together a comprehensive picture of the user's activities and intentions. Additionally, network forensics techniques are essential for investigating security incidents and cyberattacks that involve network-based activities, such as unauthorized access, data exfiltration, and malware propagation. Network forensics involves capturing and analyzing network traffic to identify anomalous patterns, malicious activities, and communication channels used by attackers. By analyzing network traffic logs, packet captures, and network device configurations, forensic examiners can identify indicators of compromise (IOCs), trace the source of attacks, and reconstruct the sequence of events leading up to a security incident. Furthermore, memory forensics techniques are critical for investigating volatile memory artifacts, such as RAM (random access memory), which contain valuable forensic evidence that can be used to identify running processes, active network connections, and malware traces. Memory forensics involves capturing and analyzing memory dumps from live systems or memory images acquired from forensic acquisitions to identify suspicious processes, malware signatures, and memory-resident artifacts. By analyzing memory dumps using specialized tools and techniques, forensic examiners can identify malicious code injections, rootkit installations, and other stealthy attacks that may evade traditional endpoint security controls. Moreover, mobile forensics techniques are essential for investigating digital evidence stored on mobile devices, such as smartphones, tablets, and wearable devices, which have become integral parts of everyday life and communication. Mobile forensics involves extracting and analyzing data from mobile devices, including call logs, text messages, emails, photos, videos, and application data, to reconstruct user activities and communications. By employing mobile forensics tools and techniques, forensic examiners can recover deleted data, bypass device locks, and extract valuable evidence from mobile devices to support criminal investigations, litigation, and incident response efforts. Additionally, malware analysis techniques are crucial for investigating malicious software (malware) samples and understanding their behavior, functionality, and impact on compromised systems. Malware analysis involves dissecting malware samples in controlled environments, such as sandbox environments or virtual machines, to identify malicious behaviors, extract indicators of compromise (IOCs), and develop mitigation strategies. By analyzing malware samples using static and dynamic analysis techniques, forensic examiners can identify malware families, uncover attack vectors, and develop signatures and detection rules to detect and mitigate malware infections effectively. Furthermore, digital forensics techniques often involve chain of custody procedures, evidence handling protocols, and legal documentation to ensure the integrity, admissibility, and reliability of digital evidence in court proceedings. Chain of custody procedures involve documenting the custody, control, and transfer of digital evidence from the time it is collected until it is presented in court, ensuring that the evidence remains intact, unaltered, and admissible in legal proceedings. By following established chain of custody procedures and evidence handling protocols, forensic examiners can maintain the integrity and reliability of digital evidence, uphold legal standards, and ensure that justice is served. In summary, digital forensics techniques are essential for investigating cybercrimes, data breaches, and other digital incidents by gathering, preserving, and analyzing digital evidence effectively. By employing disk imaging, file system analysis, network forensics, memory forensics, mobile forensics, malware analysis, and chain of custody procedures, forensic examiners can uncover valuable insights, identify perpetrators, and support legal proceedings in cases involving digital evidence.

Advanced data backup strategies are essential components of modern IT infrastructure management, providing organizations with robust and reliable solutions to protect critical data, ensure business continuity, and mitigate the risk of data loss in the event of hardware failures, cyberattacks, or natural disasters. In today's digital age, where data volumes are growing exponentially, and cyber threats are becoming increasingly sophisticated and pervasive, organizations must implement advanced data backup strategies to address evolving data protection challenges effectively. One fundamental aspect of advanced data backup strategies is the implementation of a comprehensive backup policy that defines backup objectives, data retention policies, backup frequencies, and recovery point objectives (RPOs) and recovery time objectives (RTOs). A well-defined backup policy provides clear guidelines for data protection, ensures compliance with regulatory requirements, and helps organizations align backup strategies with business priorities and risk management objectives. Moreover, advanced data backup strategies leverage a combination of backup technologies and methodologies to meet diverse data protection requirements and operational needs. These technologies may include disk-based backup, tape backup, cloud backup, and hybrid backup solutions, each offering unique advantages in terms of performance, scalability, cost-effectiveness, and data accessibility. By implementing a multi-tiered backup architecture that combines different backup technologies, organizations can optimize data protection, resilience, and recovery capabilities across the entire IT infrastructure. Additionally, advanced data backup strategies incorporate data deduplication and compression techniques to optimize storage efficiency and reduce backup storage requirements. Data deduplication eliminates redundant data blocks across backup datasets, while compression algorithms reduce the size of backup files, resulting in significant storage savings and improved backup performance. By implementing data deduplication and compression technologies, organizations can maximize backup storage utilization, reduce backup windows, and lower storage costs without compromising data protection or recovery capabilities. Furthermore, advanced data backup strategies include off-site and cloud backup solutions to provide additional layers of redundancy and disaster recovery capabilities. Off-site backup involves replicating backup data to remote locations or secondary data centers, ensuring data availability and resilience in the event of site-wide disasters, such as fires, floods, or earthquakes. Cloud backup solutions offer similar benefits by storing backup data in off-site cloud storage repositories, providing scalable, cost-effective, and geographically dispersed backup options for organizations of all sizes. By leveraging off-site and cloud backup solutions, organizations can enhance data protection, disaster recovery, and business continuity capabilities while reducing reliance on on-premises infrastructure and minimizing the risk of data loss. Moreover, advanced data backup strategies incorporate encryption and data protection mechanisms to safeguard backup data from unauthorized access, tampering, or theft. Encryption technologies encrypt backup data at rest and in transit, ensuring data confidentiality and integrity throughout the backup process. Additionally, data protection mechanisms, such as access controls, authentication, and audit trails, help organizations enforce security policies, monitor backup activities, and prevent unauthorized access to backup data. By implementing encryption and data protection measures, organizations can enhance data security, compliance, and regulatory adherence while mitigating the risk of data breaches and cyberattacks. Furthermore, advanced data backup strategies include regular backup testing, validation, and disaster recovery drills to verify the integrity and effectiveness of backup solutions and procedures. Backup testing involves performing periodic backups restores, data integrity checks, and recovery simulations to ensure that backup data is accessible, recoverable, and consistent with business requirements. Disaster recovery drills involve simulating real-world disaster scenarios, such as hardware failures, cyberattacks, or natural disasters, to test the organization's ability to recover critical systems and data within predefined RTOs and RPOs. By conducting regular backup testing and disaster recovery drills, organizations can identify and address backup-related issues, optimize recovery processes, and validate their readiness to respond to data loss incidents effectively. In summary, advanced data backup strategies are essential for organizations to protect critical data, ensure business continuity, and mitigate the risk of data loss in today's dynamic and evolving IT landscape. By implementing comprehensive backup policies, leveraging a combination of backup technologies, optimizing storage efficiency, incorporating off-site and cloud backup solutions, implementing encryption and data protection measures, and conducting regular backup testing and disaster recovery drills, organizations can enhance data protection, resilience, and recovery capabilities, safeguarding their most valuable asset against threats and ensuring operational continuity in the face of adversity.

Recovery solutions for critical data loss represent a vital aspect of modern IT infrastructure management, providing organizations with essential tools and strategies to recover lost or corrupted data and minimize the impact of data loss incidents on business operations. In today's digital age, where data serves as the lifeblood of organizations across industries, the ability to recover critical data quickly and effectively is paramount to maintaining business continuity, preserving customer trust, and avoiding financial and reputational damage. One fundamental aspect of recovery solutions for critical data loss is the implementation of robust data backup and disaster recovery strategies that ensure the continuous *availability and integrity of critical data assets. These strategies involve regular backups of essential data to secure storage repositories, such as on-premises servers, cloud platforms, or off-site data centers, to provide redundancy and resilience against data loss events, such as hardware failures, cyberattacks, or natural disasters. By maintaining up-to-date backups of critical data, organizations can restore data quickly and minimize downtime in the event of data loss incidents, ensuring uninterrupted business operations and mitigating the risk of financial losses and reputational damage. Moreover, recovery solutions for critical data loss incorporate data replication and synchronization techniques to replicate critical data in real-time or near-real-time across multiple geographically dispersed locations or data centers, providing additional layers of redundancy and fault tolerance. Data replication ensures that critical data assets are continuously synchronized and available for rapid recovery in the event of primary data loss, enabling organizations to minimize data loss and maintain operational continuity with minimal disruption. Additionally, recovery solutions for critical data loss include high availability and failover mechanisms that leverage redundant infrastructure components, such as servers, storage arrays, and network devices, to ensure uninterrupted access to critical data and applications in the event of hardware failures or system outages. High availability solutions utilize technologies, such as clustering, load balancing, and automatic failover, to detect and mitigate hardware failures or performance degradation proactively, redirecting traffic and workload to redundant infrastructure components to maintain service availability and performance. By implementing high availability and failover mechanisms, organizations can minimize downtime, improve service reliability, and ensure continuous access to critical data and applications, even in the face of hardware failures or infrastructure disruptions. Furthermore, recovery solutions for critical data loss encompass data recovery software and tools that enable organizations to recover lost or corrupted data from backup archives, storage snapshots, or disk images quickly and efficiently. Data recovery software employs advanced algorithms and techniques to scan, analyze, and recover data from damaged or inaccessible storage media, such as hard drives, solid-state drives (SSDs), or RAID arrays, restoring lost files, folders, or databases to their original state. Additionally, data recovery tools may offer features such as selective file recovery, disk imaging, and disk cloning capabilities, allowing organizations to customize recovery operations based on specific data loss scenarios and recovery requirements. Moreover, recovery solutions for critical data loss include incident response and recovery planning, which involves developing comprehensive incident response plans, playbooks, and procedures to guide organizations' response to data loss incidents effectively. Incident response and recovery planning encompass activities such as incident detection and triage, evidence collection and preservation, containment and eradication of threats, and post-incident analysis and remediation, ensuring a systematic and coordinated approach to managing data loss incidents and minimizing their impact on business operations. By developing robust incident response and recovery plans, organizations can enhance their readiness to respond to data loss incidents promptly and effectively, enabling them to mitigate the impact of data loss on business operations and reduce the risk of financial and reputational damage. Additionally, recovery solutions for critical data loss include data loss prevention (DLP) strategies and technologies that help organizations prevent data loss incidents by identifying, monitoring, and protecting sensitive data assets from unauthorized access, theft, or leakage. DLP solutions employ a combination of data discovery, classification, encryption, access controls, and monitoring capabilities to identify and protect sensitive data wherever it resides, whether it's stored on-premises, in the cloud, or in transit across networks. By implementing DLP solutions, organizations can proactively identify and mitigate data loss risks, enforce data security policies, and ensure compliance with regulatory requirements, safeguarding critical data assets from unauthorized access or exposure. In summary, recovery solutions for critical data loss are essential for organizations to recover lost or corrupted data quickly and effectively, minimize downtime, and maintain operational continuity in the face of data loss incidents. By implementing robust data backup and disaster recovery strategies, data replication and synchronization techniques, high availability and failover mechanisms,* data recovery software and tools, incident response and recovery planning, and data loss prevention strategies and technologies, organizations can enhance their resilience to data loss events, protect critical data assets, and ensure uninterrupted business operations, even in the face of adversity.

Ensuring high availability architecture is a critical consideration for organizations seeking to maintain uninterrupted access to essential services, applications, and data in today's digital landscape. High availability architecture refers to the design and implementation of IT systems and infrastructure that are resilient to hardware failures, software errors, network issues, and other disruptions, ensuring continuous availability and reliability of critical resources. In an increasingly interconnected and data-driven world, where downtime can result in significant financial losses, reputational damage, and customer dissatisfaction, high availability architecture is essential for organizations across industries, including e-commerce, finance, healthcare, and telecommunications. One fundamental aspect of ensuring high availability architecture is redundancy, which involves deploying duplicate or backup components, such as servers, storage arrays, networking devices, and power supplies, to eliminate single points of failure and mitigate the risk of downtime. Redundancy ensures that if one component fails or becomes unavailable, redundant components can seamlessly take over the workload, maintaining service availability and performance without disruption. Redundant components are typically deployed in active-passive or active-active configurations, where standby components are ready to assume the workload in the event of a failure, ensuring continuous service availability and minimizing the impact of hardware failures or maintenance activities. Additionally, ensuring high availability architecture involves implementing fault-tolerant design principles, such as fault isolation, graceful degradation, and failover mechanisms, to detect, isolate, and recover from system failures or errors automatically. Fault isolation involves partitioning systems into independent fault domains or failure zones, ensuring that failures or errors in one part of the system do not affect other parts, minimizing the impact of failures and improving system resilience. Graceful degradation involves designing systems to degrade gracefully under load or failure conditions, prioritizing critical functions and services while temporarily suspending non-essential or lower-priority functions to preserve system stability and performance. Failover mechanisms automatically redirect traffic or workload from failed or degraded components to healthy or redundant components, ensuring uninterrupted service availability and mitigating the impact of hardware failures or software errors on end-users. Moreover, ensuring high availability architecture requires implementing load balancing and traffic management solutions to distribute workload evenly across redundant or redundant components, optimizing resource utilization, performance, and scalability while ensuring fault tolerance and resilience. Load balancing solutions use algorithms, such as round-robin, least connections, or weighted distribution, to distribute incoming traffic or *workload across multiple servers or instances, preventing overloading of individual components and ensuring equitable resource allocation. Additionally, traffic management solutions employ health checks, monitoring, and dynamic routing capabilities to detect and respond to changes in system health or availability, automatically rerouting traffic away from unhealthy or overloaded components to healthy or redundant components, ensuring continuous service availability and performance optimization. Furthermore, ensuring high availability architecture involves implementing data replication and synchronization techniques to replicate critical data across multiple geographically dispersed locations or data centers, ensuring data availability, durability, and resilience in the event of data loss, corruption, or disaster. Data replication solutions replicate data in real-time or near-real-time to secondary or tertiary storage repositories, ensuring that critical data assets are continuously synchronized and available for rapid recovery in the event of primary data loss or corruption. By implementing data replication and synchronization solutions, organizations can minimize the risk of data loss, ensure data integrity and consistency, and maintain business continuity even in the face of catastrophic events such as natural disasters, cyberattacks, or infrastructure failures. Additionally, ensuring high availability architecture requires implementing comprehensive monitoring, alerting, and proactive maintenance practices to detect, diagnose, and resolve issues before they impact service availability or performance. Monitoring solutions continuously monitor system health, performance metrics, and availability indicators, providing real-time visibility into the operational status of critical components and infrastructure resources. Alerting mechanisms notify administrators or operations teams of potential issues, anomalies, or deviations from normal operating conditions, enabling proactive intervention and remediation to prevent service disruptions or performance degradation. Proactive maintenance practices, such as regular system updates, patch management, hardware upgrades, and capacity planning, ensure that infrastructure components remain up-to-date, secure, and capable of meeting evolving workload demands, minimizing the risk of downtime due to hardware failures, software vulnerabilities, or capacity constraints. In summary, ensuring high availability architecture is essential for organizations seeking to maintain uninterrupted access to essential services, applications, and data in today's digital landscape. By implementing redundancy, fault-tolerant design principles, load balancing, traffic management, data replication, synchronization, comprehensive monitoring, alerting, and proactive maintenance practices, organizations can enhance their resilience to hardware failures, software errors, network issues, and other disruptions, ensuring continuous service availability, reliability, and performance, even in the face of adversity.*

Fault tolerance troubleshooting is a critical aspect of maintaining the reliability and stability of modern IT systems, ensuring that organizations can effectively identify, diagnose, and resolve issues that may compromise fault-tolerant designs and capabilities. In today's complex and interconnected IT environments, where hardware failures, software errors, network issues, and other disruptions can occur unexpectedly, fault tolerance troubleshooting plays a crucial role in minimizing downtime, mitigating the risk of data loss, and preserving service availability and performance. One fundamental aspect of fault tolerance troubleshooting is understanding the principles and components of fault-tolerant design, which involves deploying redundant or backup components, such as servers, storage arrays, networking devices, and power supplies, to eliminate single points of failure and ensure continuous service availability. Fault-tolerant designs typically incorporate redundant components in active-passive or active-active configurations, where standby components are ready to assume the workload in the event of a failure, ensuring uninterrupted service availability and minimizing the impact of hardware failures or maintenance activities. By understanding the underlying principles of fault-tolerant design, organizations can effectively troubleshoot issues related to hardware redundancy, failover mechanisms, and fault isolation, ensuring that fault-tolerant systems operate as intended and deliver the expected levels of resilience and reliability. Additionally, fault tolerance troubleshooting involves monitoring and analyzing system health, performance metrics, and availability indicators to detect, diagnose, and resolve issues proactively before they impact service availability or performance. Monitoring solutions continuously collect and analyze data from various sources, such as hardware sensors, system logs, performance counters, and network traffic, providing real-time visibility into the operational status of critical components and infrastructure resources. By leveraging monitoring solutions, organizations can identify potential issues, anomalies, or deviations from normal operating conditions, enabling proactive intervention and remediation to prevent service disruptions or performance degradation. Moreover, fault tolerance troubleshooting requires implementing comprehensive alerting mechanisms to notify administrators or operations teams of potential issues or critical events that require immediate attention. Alerting mechanisms can be configured to trigger notifications via email, SMS, or other communication channels when predefined thresholds or conditions are met, such as CPU utilization, memory usage, disk space, or network latency exceeding predefined limits. By receiving timely alerts, administrators can quickly respond to issues, investigate root causes, and implement remediation actions to restore service availability and performance, minimizing the impact of faults or failures on business operations. Furthermore, fault tolerance troubleshooting involves analyzing system logs, event records, and error messages to identify patterns, trends, or recurring issues that may indicate underlying problems or weaknesses in fault-tolerant designs or configurations. By reviewing system logs and event records, administrators can gain insights into the *sequence of events leading up to a fault or failure, identify contributing factors, and determine appropriate corrective actions to prevent recurrence. Additionally, fault tolerance troubleshooting may involve conducting root cause analysis (RCA) to identify the underlying causes of faults or failures and implement preventive measures to address systemic issues or vulnerabilities. RCA involves systematically investigating the chain of events leading to a fault or failure, identifying contributing factors, and determining corrective actions to prevent recurrence. By conducting RCA, organizations can improve the resilience and reliability of fault-tolerant designs, mitigate the risk of future issues, and enhance overall system performance and stability. Moreover, fault tolerance troubleshooting encompasses testing and validation procedures to verify the effectiveness of fault-tolerant designs and mechanisms under various operating conditions, such as hardware failures, software errors, and network disruptions. Testing procedures may involve simulating fault scenarios, such as hardware failures, network partitions, or software crashes, and evaluating the system's response and recovery capabilities. By conducting rigorous testing and validation, organizations can identify weaknesses or vulnerabilities in fault-tolerant designs, implement corrective actions, and ensure that fault-tolerant systems operate as intended in real-world scenarios. In summary, fault tolerance troubleshooting is essential for maintaining the reliability and stability of modern IT systems, ensuring continuous service availability and performance in the face of hardware failures, software errors, network issues, and other disruptions. By understanding the principles of fault-tolerant design, monitoring system health and performance, implementing comprehensive alerting mechanisms, analyzing system logs and event records, conducting root cause analysis, and testing and validating fault-tolerant designs, organizations can effectively identify, diagnose, and resolve issues that may compromise fault tolerance capabilities, minimizing downtime and preserving service continuity.*

Advanced scripting techniques represent a cornerstone of modern IT automation and system administration, enabling organizations to streamline workflows, automate repetitive tasks, and achieve greater efficiency and consistency in managing complex IT environments. In today's dynamic and rapidly evolving digital landscape, where the volume and complexity of IT operations continue to grow, advanced scripting techniques play a crucial role in empowering IT professionals to handle diverse challenges and achieve their goals more effectively. One fundamental aspect of advanced scripting techniques is mastering scripting languages such as Python, PowerShell, Bash, or Ruby, which provide powerful and flexible tools for automating a wide range of tasks across different platforms and environments. These scripting languages offer rich libraries, modules, and frameworks that support various automation scenarios, including system administration, configuration management, deployment automation, data processing, and web development, among others. By mastering scripting languages, IT professionals can leverage their capabilities to create custom scripts, utilities, and automation workflows tailored to their specific needs, improving productivity, reducing manual errors, and accelerating time-to-resolution for IT operations. Additionally, advanced scripting techniques involve understanding and applying programming concepts such as variables, data types, control structures, functions, and error handling, which are essential for writing robust, maintainable, and efficient scripts. Variables allow scripts to store and manipulate data dynamically, while data types define the type and format of data that scripts can handle, ensuring data integrity and consistency. Control structures, such as loops and conditional statements, enable scripts to execute commands or perform actions based on predefined conditions or criteria, providing flexibility and logic to automation workflows. Functions encapsulate reusable code blocks or operations, allowing scripts to modularize complex tasks and promote code reuse, maintainability, and readability. Error handling mechanisms enable scripts to detect, handle, and recover from errors or exceptions gracefully, ensuring robustness and reliability in automation workflows. Moreover, advanced scripting techniques involve leveraging scripting frameworks and libraries, such as Ansible, Puppet, Chef, or SaltStack, which provide higher-level abstractions, tools, and components for automating IT infrastructure management and configuration. These frameworks offer pre-built modules, templates, and workflows for common automation tasks, such as provisioning servers, configuring network devices, deploying applications, and managing software packages, enabling organizations to accelerate automation initiatives and achieve faster time-to-value. By leveraging scripting frameworks, IT professionals can streamline the development, deployment, and management of automation workflows, reduce scripting effort, and increase the scalability and repeatability of automation processes. Furthermore, advanced scripting techniques encompass integrating scripts with other automation tools and technologies, such as version control systems, continuous integration/continuous deployment (CI/CD) pipelines, configuration management databases (CMDBs), and monitoring and alerting platforms. Integration with version control systems, such as Git, enables IT professionals to manage script versions, collaborate with team members, and track changes systematically, ensuring code quality, consistency, and traceability across automation workflows. Integration with CI/CD pipelines automates the testing, building, and deployment of scripts, ensuring that changes are validated and propagated automatically to production environments, reducing deployment errors and accelerating time-to-production. Integration with CMDBs provides visibility into the configuration and dependencies of IT assets, enabling scripts to dynamically adapt and respond to changes in the environment, ensuring consistency and compliance with organizational standards. Integration with monitoring and alerting platforms enables scripts to detect, respond to, and remediate issues proactively, ensuring the reliability and availability of IT services and infrastructure. Moreover, advanced scripting techniques involve optimizing scripts for performance, scalability, and resource efficiency, which are critical considerations for managing large-scale, distributed, or resource-

constrained environments. Optimization techniques may include minimizing script execution time by optimizing algorithms, reducing unnecessary I/O operations, or parallelizing tasks to leverage multi-core processors and concurrency. Additionally, optimization techniques may involve optimizing memory usage by managing data structures efficiently, minimizing memory allocations, or implementing caching mechanisms to reduce overhead and improve script performance. Furthermore, optimization techniques may involve optimizing resource usage by managing system resources, such as CPU, memory, disk, and network bandwidth, effectively, ensuring that scripts operate within resource constraints and do not impact other applications or services negatively. In summary, advanced scripting techniques play a crucial role in modern IT automation and system administration, enabling organizations to streamline workflows, automate repetitive tasks, and achieve greater efficiency and consistency in managing complex IT environments. By mastering scripting languages, understanding programming concepts, leveraging scripting frameworks and libraries, integrating with other automation tools and technologies, and optimizing scripts for performance, scalability, and resource efficiency, IT professionals can maximize the value and impact of automation initiatives, drive operational excellence, and deliver superior business outcomes in today's fast-paced and competitive digital landscape.

Implementing automated troubleshooting workflows is a pivotal endeavor for modern organizations seeking to *streamline IT operations, enhance productivity, and improve service delivery in today's dynamic and fast-paced digital landscape. Automated troubleshooting workflows empower IT teams to detect, diagnose, and resolve issues swiftly and efficiently, minimizing downtime, optimizing resource utilization, and ensuring the reliability and availability of critical IT services and infrastructure. One fundamental aspect of implementing automated troubleshooting workflows is identifying and prioritizing common issues and pain points that frequently affect IT operations and service delivery. By analyzing historical data, incident reports, and service tickets, organizations can gain insights into recurring issues, patterns, and trends, enabling them to prioritize automation efforts and focus on areas where automation can deliver the most significant value and impact. Common issues may include software errors, hardware failures, network outages, performance degradation, security vulnerabilities, and configuration errors, among others, which can disrupt business operations, affect user productivity, and degrade the customer experience if left unresolved. By prioritizing automation efforts based on the frequency, severity, and business impact of common issues, organizations can maximize the effectiveness and ROI of automated troubleshooting workflows, addressing critical pain points and delivering tangible benefits to the business. Additionally, implementing automated troubleshooting workflows involves leveraging monitoring and alerting solutions to detect and notify IT teams of potential issues or anomalies in real-time. Monitoring solutions continuously collect and analyze data from various sources, such as servers, network devices, applications,* and databases, providing insights into system health, performance metrics, and availability indicators. By configuring monitoring solutions to generate alerts when predefined thresholds or conditions are met, IT teams can proactively identify and respond to issues before they escalate into full-blown outages or service disruptions. Alerts can be configured to trigger notifications via email, SMS, or other communication channels, ensuring that IT teams are promptly notified of critical events requiring attention and intervention. Moreover, implementing automated troubleshooting workflows involves developing and deploying diagnostic scripts, utilities, and automation tools that can detect, diagnose, and remediate common issues autonomously. Diagnostic scripts leverage scripting languages, such as Python, PowerShell, Bash, or Ruby, to execute predefined diagnostic tests, collect relevant system information, and analyze log files, event records, and error messages to identify the root cause of issues accurately. By automating diagnostic tasks, organizations can accelerate the troubleshooting process, reduce manual effort, and improve the accuracy and consistency of issue identification and resolution. Furthermore, implementing automated troubleshooting workflows requires integrating diagnostic scripts with existing IT management and ticketing systems to facilitate seamless incident response and resolution. Integration with IT management systems, such as IT service management (ITSM) platforms, enables diagnostic scripts to create and update incident tickets automatically, providing IT teams with a centralized repository for tracking and managing ongoing issues and escalations. Integration with ticketing systems streamlines the incident resolution process, *ensuring that diagnostic findings and remediation actions are documented, tracked, and communicated effectively, reducing the time-to-resolution and improving service levels. Additionally, implementing automated troubleshooting workflows involves establishing escalation and remediation procedures to handle complex or unresolved issues that cannot be resolved automatically. Escalation procedures define the hierarchy and roles of IT personnel responsible for handling different types of issues, specifying escalation paths and communication channels for escalating issues to higher-level support tiers or subject matter experts. Remediation procedures outline the steps and actions required to resolve issues that cannot be resolved automatically, such as manual interventions, hardware replacements, software patches, or configuration changes. By establishing clear escalation and remediation procedures, organizations can ensure that issues are addressed promptly and effectively, minimizing the impact on business operations and user experience. Moreover, implementing automated troubleshooting workflows requires continuous monitoring, optimization, and refinement to adapt to evolving IT environments, technologies, and business requirements. Organizations must regularly review and update diagnostic scripts, automation tools, and escalation procedures to reflect changes in system configurations, application dependencies, and service level agreements (SLAs). By monitoring the performance and effectiveness of automated troubleshooting workflows, organizations can identify areas for improvement, refine automation logic, and optimize diagnostic scripts to enhance accuracy, efficiency, and scalability. Furthermore, organizations can leverage machine learning and artificial intelligence (AI) technologies to augment automated troubleshooting workflows, enabling predictive analytics, anomaly detection, and proactive remediation of issues before they impact service availability or performance. By analyzing historical data and patterns, machine learning algorithms can identify potential issues, predict future failures, and recommend preventive actions, enabling organizations to anticipate and mitigate risks proactively. In summary, implementing automated troubleshooting workflows is essential for modern organizations seeking to enhance IT operations, improve service delivery, and ensure the reliability and availability of critical IT services and infrastructure. By prioritizing common issues, leveraging monitoring and alerting solutions, developing diagnostic scripts, integrating with IT management systems, establishing escalation and remediation procedures, and embracing continuous improvement and innovation, organizations can optimize the effectiveness and efficiency of automated troubleshooting workflows, drive operational excellence, and deliver superior business outcomes in today's digital era.*

Real-world examples of expert troubleshooting provide invaluable insights into the practical application of troubleshooting methodologies, techniques, and best practices in diverse IT environments and scenarios. These examples illustrate how IT professionals diagnose and resolve complex issues, overcome challenges, and deliver effective solutions to ensure the reliability, performance, and security of IT systems and services. One illustrative example of expert troubleshooting involves diagnosing and resolving network connectivity issues in a large enterprise environment. Suppose users report intermittent connectivity issues when accessing network resources or applications. In that case, IT professionals may begin by gathering information about the reported symptoms, such as the frequency and duration of the connectivity problems, affected users, and types of network activities impacted. Using network monitoring tools, packet analyzers, and log files, IT professionals can analyze network traffic, identify patterns, and pinpoint potential bottlenecks or points of failure. In some cases, the issue may stem from misconfigured network devices, such as routers, switches, or firewalls, causing packet loss, latency, or congestion. By examining device configurations, routing tables, and access control lists (ACLs), IT professionals can identify and rectify configuration errors, optimize network settings, and improve traffic flow to restore connectivity and alleviate performance issues. Another real-world example of expert troubleshooting involves diagnosing and resolving performance degradation issues in a virtualized server environment. Suppose users experience sluggish performance or responsiveness when accessing virtualized applications or services hosted on hypervisor platforms. In that case, IT professionals may investigate potential causes, such as resource contention, overutilization, or configuration issues within the virtualized infrastructure. Using performance monitoring tools, hypervisor management consoles, and system logs, IT professionals can analyze resource utilization metrics, such as CPU, memory, disk, and network usage, across virtual machines (VMs) and host servers. By identifying VMs experiencing high resource utilization or contention, IT professionals can rebalance workloads, adjust resource allocations, or migrate VMs to less congested hosts to improve performance and alleviate bottlenecks. Additionally, IT professionals may optimize hypervisor settings, such as memory ballooning, CPU scheduling, and disk caching, to enhance virtual machine performance and responsiveness further. A third real-world example of expert troubleshooting involves diagnosing and remediating cybersecurity incidents, such as malware infections, data breaches, or unauthorized access attempts. Suppose an organization detects unusual network activity, suspicious file modifications, or unauthorized user logins indicative of a security breach. In that case, IT security professionals must respond promptly to contain the incident, investigate the root cause, and implement remediation measures to prevent further damage or data loss. Using security information and event management (SIEM) tools, intrusion detection systems (IDS), and endpoint security solutions, IT security professionals can analyze security logs, network traffic, and system activity to identify indicators of compromise (IOCs) and attack vectors. By correlating security events, analyzing malware samples, and tracing the attacker's movements, IT security professionals can determine the scope and severity of the security incident, assess the impact on critical assets, and prioritize response actions accordingly. Remediation measures may include isolating compromised systems, applying security patches, updating antivirus signatures, resetting compromised credentials, and enhancing security controls to prevent future incidents. Furthermore, real-world examples of expert troubleshooting often highlight the importance of collaboration, communication, and knowledge sharing among IT teams and stakeholders. In complex troubleshooting scenarios, IT professionals may need to collaborate across different departments, such as networking, systems administration, security, and application support, to leverage their expertise and perspectives in diagnosing and resolving issues effectively. By fostering a culture of collaboration and knowledge sharing, organizations can harness the collective intelligence and experience of their IT teams to tackle challenges more efficiently and innovate solutions that drive business success. Additionally, documenting troubleshooting processes, solutions, and lessons learned from real-world examples enables organizations to build a knowledge base of best practices, troubleshooting strategies, and problem-solving techniques that can be leveraged in future incidents. By capturing and codifying expertise, organizations can accelerate the resolution of similar issues, reduce downtime, and enhance the overall resilience and reliability of IT systems and services. In summary, real-world examples of expert troubleshooting offer valuable insights into the application of troubleshooting methodologies, techniques, and best practices in diverse IT environments and scenarios. By examining how IT professionals diagnose and resolve complex issues, overcome challenges, and collaborate effectively, organizations can learn from past experiences, improve their troubleshooting capabilities, and enhance the reliability, performance, and security of their IT infrastructure and services.

Analyzing successful troubleshooting strategies provides invaluable insights into the methods, techniques, and approaches that IT professionals employ to diagnose and resolve complex issues effectively in diverse IT environments. By examining successful troubleshooting cases and dissecting the strategies employed, organizations can identify patterns, best practices, and lessons learned that can inform and improve their own troubleshooting processes. One key aspect of analyzing successful troubleshooting strategies is understanding the importance of thorough problem analysis and diagnosis. Successful troubleshooting often begins with *a systematic approach to gathering information, understanding symptoms, and identifying potential root causes. IT professionals must leverage diagnostic tools, log files, system metrics, and user reports to gain a comprehensive understanding of the issue's scope, impact, and underlying causes. By conducting thorough problem analysis, IT professionals can narrow down potential root causes, prioritize troubleshooting efforts, and develop targeted solutions that address the underlying issues effectively. Additionally, successful troubleshooting strategies often involve leveraging a combination of technical expertise, critical thinking, and creativity to identify and implement innovative solutions. IT professionals must draw upon their knowledge of IT systems, networks, applications, and technologies to diagnose and resolve issues accurately. However, successful troubleshooting also requires the ability to think outside the box, explore alternative hypotheses, and experiment with different approaches to problem-solving. By embracing creativity and lateral thinking, IT professionals can uncover hidden issues, uncover unconventional solutions, and overcome obstacles that may impede the troubleshooting process. Moreover, successful troubleshooting strategies emphasize the importance of collaboration and communication among IT teams, stakeholders, and subject matter experts. Complex issues often require interdisciplinary expertise and collaboration across different functional areas, such as networking, systems administration, security, and application development. IT professionals must work together effectively, share* information, and leverage each other's strengths to diagnose and resolve issues collaboratively. By fostering a culture of collaboration and knowledge sharing, organizations can harness the collective intelligence and experience of their teams to tackle challenges more effectively and innovate solutions that drive business success. Furthermore, successful troubleshooting strategies prioritize proactive monitoring, continuous improvement, and preventive maintenance to prevent recurring issues and minimize downtime. IT professionals must implement robust monitoring solutions that provide real-time visibility into IT systems, applications, and services, enabling them to detect and address issues before they escalate into critical problems. By proactively monitoring key performance indicators, system metrics, and event logs, IT professionals can identify potential issues early, implement preventive measures, and mitigate risks before they impact business operations. Additionally, successful troubleshooting strategies involve documenting and sharing lessons learned from past troubleshooting experiences to improve future responses to similar issues. By maintaining a centralized repository of troubleshooting knowledge, best practices, and solutions, organizations can accelerate the resolution of issues, reduce downtime, and enhance the overall resilience and reliability of IT systems and services. Furthermore, successful troubleshooting strategies emphasize the importance of continuous learning, training, and professional development to keep IT professionals abreast of the latest technologies, tools, and techniques in the field. By investing in ongoing training and skills development, organizations can equip their IT teams with the knowledge, expertise, and capabilities needed to tackle complex issues effectively and adapt to evolving IT environments. Moreover, successful troubleshooting strategies require organizations to foster a culture of accountability, ownership, and empowerment among IT professionals. IT teams must take ownership of issues, drive resolution efforts proactively, and hold themselves accountable for delivering results. By empowering IT professionals to take initiative, make decisions, and act decisively, organizations can accelerate the resolution of issues, improve service levels, and enhance customer satisfaction. In summary, analyzing successful troubleshooting strategies offers valuable insights into the methods, techniques, and approaches that IT professionals employ to diagnose and resolve complex issues effectively in diverse IT environments. By embracing thorough problem analysis, leveraging technical expertise and creativity, fostering collaboration and communication, prioritizing proactive monitoring and preventive maintenance, documenting lessons learned, investing in continuous learning and professional development, and fostering a culture of accountability and empowerment, organizations can optimize their troubleshooting capabilities and ensure the reliability, performance, and security of their IT infrastructure and services.

BOOK 4
BEYOND THE BASICS
SPECIALIZED APPROACHES IN IT TROUBLESHOOTING

ROB BOTWRIGHT

Enterprise Network Architecture Analysis is a critical process that involves evaluating, assessing, and optimizing the design, structure, and components of an organization's network infrastructure to meet business requirements, enhance performance, and ensure scalability, security, and reliability. In today's digital age, where connectivity is paramount for business operations, analyzing enterprise network architecture is essential for organizations to adapt to evolving technological trends, support emerging business needs, and stay competitive in the marketplace. One key aspect of enterprise network architecture analysis is understanding the current state of the network infrastructure, including its topology, components, protocols, and configurations. IT professionals must conduct thorough audits and assessments to document existing network assets, such as routers, switches, firewalls, servers, and endpoints, and analyze their interconnections, dependencies, and traffic patterns. By gaining visibility into the network's architecture and infrastructure, organizations can identify areas of strengths, weaknesses, and inefficiencies that may impact performance, security, or compliance. Additionally, enterprise network architecture analysis involves evaluating the scalability and flexibility of the network design to accommodate growth, expansion, and changing business requirements. IT professionals must assess the network's capacity, bandwidth, and resource utilization to determine whether it can support increasing traffic volumes, new applications, or additional users without degradation in performance or reliability. By identifying potential scalability bottlenecks or limitations, organizations can proactively plan for network upgrades, expansions, or optimizations to ensure that the network can scale effectively to meet future demands. Moreover, enterprise network architecture analysis encompasses evaluating the security posture of the network infrastructure to identify vulnerabilities, risks, and compliance gaps. IT professionals must assess the effectiveness of existing security controls, such as firewalls, intrusion detection systems (IDS), and encryption protocols, in safeguarding sensitive data, protecting against cyber threats, and complying with industry regulations and standards. By conducting security assessments, penetration tests, and vulnerability scans, organizations can uncover weaknesses in the network's defenses, such as misconfigurations, outdated firmware, or unpatched vulnerabilities, and prioritize remediation efforts to mitigate risks and strengthen security posture. Furthermore, enterprise network architecture analysis involves assessing the performance and reliability of critical network services and applications to ensure optimal user experience and productivity. IT professionals must monitor key performance indicators (KPIs), such as latency, packet loss, and throughput, to identify performance bottlenecks, congestion points, or quality of service (QoS) issues that may impact application delivery or user satisfaction. By optimizing network configurations, traffic routing, and resource allocation, organizations can enhance application performance, minimize downtime, and improve user productivity, resulting in a more efficient and responsive network environment. Additionally, enterprise network architecture analysis encompasses evaluating the resilience and fault tolerance of the network design to withstand disruptions, failures, or disasters gracefully. IT professionals must assess the redundancy, failover mechanisms, and disaster recovery plans implemented within the network infrastructure to ensure business continuity and data integrity in the event of unforeseen events, such as hardware failures, natural disasters, or cyber attacks. By implementing robust redundancy schemes, geographic diversity, and backup strategies, organizations can minimize downtime, mitigate data loss, and maintain operational continuity, even in the face of adverse conditions or catastrophic events. Moreover, enterprise network architecture analysis involves aligning the network infrastructure with business objectives, priorities, and growth strategies to maximize return on investment (ROI) and business value. IT professionals must collaborate closely with stakeholders, department heads, and business leaders to understand their requirements, challenges, and strategic initiatives and translate them into actionable network design principles and guidelines. By aligning network architecture with business goals, organizations can ensure that network investments support strategic objectives, drive innovation, and enable digital transformation initiatives, resulting in a more agile, responsive, and competitive enterprise. In summary, enterprise network architecture analysis is a multifaceted process that involves evaluating, assessing, and optimizing the design, structure, and components of an organization's network infrastructure to meet business requirements, enhance performance, and ensure scalability, security, and reliability. By conducting thorough assessments, identifying areas for improvement, and implementing targeted optimizations and enhancements, organizations can build a robust, agile, and resilient network architecture that supports their current and future business needs effectively. Advanced troubleshooting strategies for large-scale networks are essential for maintaining the performance, reliability, and security of complex network infrastructures that support extensive user populations, diverse applications, and distributed locations. In today's interconnected world, where enterprises rely heavily on digital technologies for their daily operations, the ability to diagnose and resolve network issues efficiently and effectively is paramount for ensuring uninterrupted business continuity and delivering a seamless user experience. One of the primary challenges in troubleshooting large-scale networks is the sheer complexity and diversity of network components, configurations, and traffic patterns. With numerous routers, switches, firewalls, servers, endpoints, and interconnected subsystems spanning multiple geographic locations and environments, diagnosing issues can be daunting. To address this challenge, advanced troubleshooting strategies leverage comprehensive network monitoring and analytics tools that provide real-time visibility into network traffic, performance metrics, and device health status. By aggregating and analyzing telemetry data from various network devices and sources, IT professionals can gain actionable insights into network behavior, identify anomalies, and proactively detect and diagnose potential issues before they escalate. Additionally, advanced troubleshooting strategies for large-scale networks emphasize the importance of leveraging automation and orchestration to streamline troubleshooting workflows and expedite issue resolution. Automation tools, such as network configuration management systems, orchestration platforms, and scripting frameworks, enable IT teams to automate repetitive tasks, standardize configuration changes, and deploy remediation actions rapidly across the network infrastructure. By automating routine troubleshooting tasks, organizations can reduce manual effort, minimize human errors, and accelerate response times, thereby improving operational efficiency and agility. Furthermore, advanced troubleshooting strategies for large-scale networks prioritize the implementation of proactive monitoring and predictive analytics capabilities to anticipate and prevent network issues before they impact users or business operations. Proactive monitoring solutions continuously monitor key performance indicators (KPIs), such as latency, packet loss, and bandwidth utilization, and use machine learning algorithms to analyze historical trends and predict future network behavior. By leveraging predictive analytics, IT professionals can identify potential performance bottlenecks, capacity constraints, or security vulnerabilities early on and take preemptive measures to mitigate risks and optimize network performance. Moreover, advanced troubleshooting strategies for large-scale networks involve adopting a holistic and collaborative approach to problem-solving that encourages cross-functional collaboration, knowledge sharing, and communication among IT teams, stakeholders, and vendors. Complex network issues often require expertise from multiple domains, such as networking, systems administration, security, and application development, to diagnose and resolve effectively. By fostering a culture of collaboration and teamwork, organizations can leverage the collective intelligence and experience of their teams to tackle challenges more efficiently and innovate solutions that address root causes comprehensively. Additionally, advanced troubleshooting strategies for large-scale networks emphasize the importance of implementing robust change management and configuration control processes to minimize the risk of unintended consequences or disruptions during troubleshooting activities. Changes to network configurations, policies, or settings can inadvertently introduce new issues or exacerbate existing ones if not properly planned, documented, and tested. Therefore, IT professionals must adhere to strict change control procedures, conduct thorough impact assessments, and follow *established best practices to ensure that changes are implemented safely and efficiently without impacting network stability or performance. Furthermore, advanced troubleshooting strategies for large-scale networks recognize the importance of continuous learning, training, and professional development to keep IT teams abreast of the latest technologies, tools, and techniques in the field. As network technologies evolve rapidly and new threats emerge, IT professionals must stay vigilant, adaptable, and proactive in acquiring new skills and knowledge to address emerging challenges effectively. By investing in ongoing training programs, certifications, and hands-on workshops, organizations can empower their IT teams to stay ahead of the curve, enhance their troubleshooting capabilities, and deliver value-added solutions that meet evolving business needs. In summary, advanced troubleshooting strategies for large-scale networks are essential for maintaining the performance, reliability, and security of modern enterprise networks. By leveraging comprehensive monitoring and analytics tools, automation and orchestration capabilities, proactive monitoring and predictive analytics, collaborative problem-solving approaches, robust change management processes, and continuous learning and development initiatives, organizations can optimize their troubleshooting capabilities and ensure the resilience and agility of their network infrastructure in the face of evolving challenges and demands.*

Server performance monitoring and optimization are critical processes in managing and maintaining the efficiency, reliability, and scalability of IT infrastructures that rely on server-based applications and services. In today's digital landscape, where businesses depend heavily on servers to deliver mission-critical applications, ensuring optimal server performance is essential for meeting user expectations, maximizing productivity, and driving business growth. Server performance monitoring involves the continuous observation and analysis of various metrics, such as CPU utilization, memory usage, disk I/O, network traffic, and application response times, to assess the health and performance of server hardware and software components. By monitoring these key performance indicators (KPIs) in real-time or at regular intervals, IT professionals can identify performance bottlenecks, resource constraints, and anomalies that may impact server performance and user experience. Furthermore, server performance monitoring tools provide insights into historical trends, patterns, and usage trends, enabling IT teams to forecast future capacity requirements, plan for upgrades, and optimize resource allocation proactively. Additionally, server performance optimization involves implementing strategies and techniques to improve server efficiency, responsiveness, and throughput while minimizing resource wastage, latency, and downtime. One approach to server performance optimization is capacity planning, which involves forecasting future workload demands, assessing current resource utilization trends, and identifying potential capacity constraints or bottlenecks. By accurately predicting future resource needs and scaling server infrastructure accordingly, organizations can ensure that servers have sufficient capacity to handle workload spikes, accommodate growth, and maintain optimal performance levels. Another key aspect of server performance optimization is tuning server configurations and settings to optimize resource utilization, mitigate performance bottlenecks, and enhance overall system responsiveness. This may involve adjusting operating system parameters, fine-tuning application settings, optimizing database queries, or implementing caching mechanisms to improve data access times and reduce latency. Moreover, server performance optimization encompasses implementing proactive maintenance practices, such as patch management, firmware updates, and hardware refresh cycles, to address known vulnerabilities, enhance system stability, and optimize performance. By keeping server software and hardware up to date with the latest security patches, bug fixes, and optimizations, organizations can minimize the risk of security breaches, system crashes, and performance degradation caused by outdated or vulnerable components. Additionally, server performance optimization involves leveraging advanced technologies, such as virtualization, containerization, and cloud computing, to optimize resource utilization, enhance scalability, and streamline server management. Virtualization technologies enable organizations to consolidate multiple virtual servers onto a single physical host, maximizing hardware utilization and reducing operational costs. Containerization technologies, such as Docker and Kubernetes, provide lightweight, portable, and scalable deployment options for applications, enabling organizations to achieve greater efficiency and agility in server resource allocation and management. Furthermore, cloud computing platforms offer on-demand access to scalable and elastic compute resources, allowing organizations to scale server infrastructure dynamically to meet fluctuating workload demands and optimize cost-effectiveness. Moreover, server performance optimization involves implementing robust monitoring and alerting systems to proactively detect and address performance issues before they impact users or business operations. By leveraging monitoring tools that provide real-time visibility into server performance metrics, IT teams can identify anomalies, set performance thresholds, and receive alerts when performance deviates from expected norms. Additionally, server performance optimization encompasses implementing workload balancing and load distribution mechanisms to evenly distribute workloads across multiple servers, optimize resource utilization, and improve fault tolerance and resilience. By distributing workloads strategically based on server capacity, availability, and performance characteristics,

*organizations can prevent resource bottlenecks, minimize downtime, and ensure high availability and reliability of server-based applications and services. Furthermore, server performance optimization involves implementing efficient data storage and retrieval strategies to minimize disk I/O latency, reduce storage costs, and improve overall system performance. This may involve implementing data caching mechanisms, optimizing database indexes, or using solid-state drives (SSDs) to accelerate data access times and improve application responsiveness. Additionally, server performance optimization encompasses implementing security best practices, such as access controls, encryption, and intrusion detection systems, to protect server resources from unauthorized access, data breaches, and cyber threats. By securing servers and data against potential security risks and vulnerabilities, organizations can safeguard the integrity, confidentiality, and availability of critical business information and assets. In summary, server performance monitoring and optimization are essential processes for maintaining the efficiency, reliability, and scalability of server infrastructure in modern IT environments. By continuously monitoring server performance metrics, implementing proactive optimization strategies, leveraging advanced technologies, and adhering to best practices, organizations can ensure optimal server performance, maximize resource utilization, and deliver seamless user experiences while minimizing downtime, risks, and costs.
Infrastructure debugging techniques for complex*

environments are indispensable for identifying, diagnosing, and resolving issues that arise in intricate IT infrastructures comprising diverse components, configurations, and dependencies. In today's dynamic and interconnected digital landscape, where organizations rely heavily on complex infrastructures to support mission-critical applications and services, effective debugging is essential for ensuring optimal performance, reliability, and security. Debugging complex environments involves a systematic approach that combines diagnostic tools, methodologies, and best practices to pinpoint the root causes of issues and implement targeted solutions efficiently. One of the fundamental aspects of infrastructure debugging is thorough documentation and understanding of the environment's architecture, including network topology, hardware configurations, software components, and interdependencies. IT professionals must have a comprehensive understanding of the infrastructure's design and functionality to effectively troubleshoot issues and identify potential points of failure or misconfiguration. Additionally, infrastructure debugging relies on the use of specialized diagnostic tools and utilities to gather data, analyze system behavior, and identify anomalies or errors. These tools may include network analyzers, system monitoring software, log analysis tools, performance profiling utilities, and debugging frameworks, among others. By leveraging these tools, IT teams can collect valuable information about the environment's state, performance metrics, and operational parameters, enabling them to diagnose issues accurately and efficiently. Moreover, infrastructure debugging techniques emphasize the importance of systematic problem-solving methodologies, such as root cause analysis (RCA), fault tree analysis (FTA), and the scientific method, to methodically investigate and resolve issues. These methodologies provide structured frameworks for identifying potential causes of problems, testing hypotheses, and validating solutions through empirical evidence. By following a systematic approach to debugging, IT professionals can avoid jumping to conclusions, ensure thorough investigation of all possible causes, and make informed decisions based on evidence and data. Furthermore, infrastructure debugging techniques involve collaboration and communication among cross-functional teams, including network engineers, system administrators, developers, and business stakeholders. Complex infrastructure issues often require expertise from multiple domains, and effective communication and collaboration are essential for sharing knowledge, exchanging ideas, and coordinating efforts to resolve issues collaboratively. By fostering a culture of collaboration and teamwork, organizations can leverage the collective expertise and insights of their teams to accelerate the debugging process and implement robust solutions effectively. Additionally, infrastructure debugging techniques emphasize the importance of continuous monitoring and proactive maintenance to prevent issues from occurring in the first place. By implementing robust monitoring solutions that provide real-time visibility into system performance, health, and security, organizations can detect anomalies, deviations, or potential issues early on and take preemptive action to address them before they impact operations. Moreover, infrastructure debugging involves leveraging automation and orchestration to streamline troubleshooting workflows, automate routine tasks, and expedite issue resolution. Automation tools, such as configuration management systems, orchestration platforms, and scripting frameworks, enable IT teams to automate repetitive tasks, standardize configurations, and deploy remediation actions rapidly across the infrastructure. By automating routine debugging tasks, organizations can reduce manual effort, minimize human errors, and improve overall operational efficiency. Furthermore, infrastructure debugging techniques emphasize the importance of maintaining comprehensive documentation of debugging processes, findings, and resolutions to facilitate knowledge sharing, replication, and future troubleshooting efforts. Detailed documentation ensures that valuable insights and lessons learned from debugging activities are captured, preserved, and disseminated across the organization, enabling IT teams to build institutional knowledge and improve their debugging capabilities over time. Additionally, infrastructure debugging techniques involve implementing robust testing and validation procedures to verify the effectiveness of proposed solutions and ensure that they do not introduce new issues or regressions into the environment. By conducting thorough testing and validation, *organizations can mitigate the risk of unintended consequences, validate the correctness of fixes, and ensure the stability and reliability of the infrastructure post-debugging. In summary, infrastructure debugging techniques are essential for identifying, diagnosing, and resolving issues in complex IT environments. By combining systematic problem-solving methodologies, specialized diagnostic tools, collaboration and communication, continuous monitoring and proactive maintenance, automation and orchestration, documentation, and testing and validation, organizations can effectively debug their infrastructure, optimize performance, and ensure the reliability and resilience of their IT systems.*

Strategies for integrating diverse software systems are crucial in today's interconnected digital landscape, where organizations rely on a multitude of applications, platforms, and technologies to support their business operations. Integration involves the seamless exchange of data, functionality, and processes between disparate software systems to enhance collaboration, streamline workflows, and improve overall efficiency. Successful integration requires careful planning, implementation, and management to ensure compatibility, interoperability, and scalability across the entire software ecosystem. One of the fundamental strategies for integrating diverse software systems is adopting a modular and standards-based approach to system design and development. By breaking down complex systems into smaller, reusable components and adhering to industry standards and protocols, organizations can facilitate interoperability and simplify integration efforts. Modular architectures, such as service-oriented architecture (SOA) or microservices architecture, enable organizations to decouple functionality into independent services that can communicate with each other through well-defined interfaces, making it easier to integrate and extend software systems as needed. Additionally, leveraging industry-standard protocols and data formats, such as

HTTP, RESTful APIs, JSON, or XML, ensures compatibility and interoperability between different software systems, enabling seamless data exchange and communication. Another key strategy for integrating diverse software systems is implementing middleware or integration platforms that act as intermediaries between disparate systems, facilitating communication, data transformation, and orchestration. Middleware solutions, such as enterprise service buses (ESBs), integration brokers, or message queuing systems, provide a centralized platform for managing integration workflows, translating between different data formats and protocols, and ensuring reliable message delivery across heterogeneous environments. By deploying middleware, organizations can abstract the complexities of integration, simplify connectivity between systems, and achieve greater flexibility and scalability in managing integration processes. Furthermore, adopting an event-driven architecture (EDA) can enhance the flexibility and responsiveness of software systems by enabling real-time event processing and asynchronous communication between components. In an event-driven architecture, software systems generate and consume events to trigger actions, propagate updates, or communicate changes in state, allowing for loosely coupled and highly scalable integration scenarios. By embracing event-driven design principles, organizations can build more resilient, adaptive, and responsive software systems that can seamlessly integrate with external services, react to changing business requirements, and scale to meet growing demands.

Additionally, leveraging cloud-native integration solutions, such as iPaaS (integration platform as a service) or API management platforms, can simplify and accelerate the integration of diverse software systems across hybrid and multi-cloud environments. Cloud-native integration platforms provide pre-built connectors, APIs, and tools for integrating with popular SaaS applications, cloud services, and on-premises systems, enabling organizations to rapidly deploy, configure, and manage integrations without the need for extensive custom development or infrastructure investment. Moreover, adopting a data-driven approach to integration can help organizations derive actionable insights, drive informed decision-making, and unlock new business opportunities by leveraging data from disparate sources and systems. By implementing data integration and analytics solutions, such as data warehouses, data lakes, or master data management (MDM) systems, organizations can consolidate, cleanse, and harmonize data from various sources to create a single, unified view of their business operations and customers. This unified data model enables organizations to perform advanced analytics, generate meaningful insights, and derive value from their data assets, driving innovation and competitive advantage. Furthermore, embracing agile development practices and DevOps methodologies can accelerate the integration of diverse software systems by promoting collaboration, automation, and continuous delivery across development, operations, and integration teams. By adopting agile principles, such as iterative development, frequent releases, and cross-functional teams, organizations can reduce time-to-market, mitigate risks, and adapt quickly to changing integration requirements and priorities. Additionally, implementing DevOps practices, such as infrastructure as code (IaC), automated testing, and continuous integration/continuous deployment (CI/CD), enables organizations to automate and streamline the deployment and management of integration solutions, ensuring consistency, reliability, and scalability across development, testing, and production environments. In summary, strategies for integrating diverse software systems are essential for organizations seeking to harness the full potential of their software investments and create cohesive, interoperable, and scalable IT ecosystems. By adopting modular and standards-based architectures, leveraging middleware and integration platforms, embracing event-driven and cloud-native integration solutions, adopting a data-driven approach, and embracing agile and DevOps practices, organizations can streamline integration efforts, enhance collaboration, and unlock new opportunities for innovation and growth in today's digital economy. Resolving compatibility issues in software integration is a critical aspect of ensuring the smooth operation and interoperability of diverse applications, platforms, and technologies within an organization's IT ecosystem. Compatibility issues often arise when integrating software systems that have different architectures, dependencies, or versions, leading to conflicts, errors, and disruptions in functionality. Addressing these issues *requires a systematic approach that involves identifying compatibility challenges, implementing targeted solutions, and testing thoroughly to validate compatibility across the entire integration landscape. One common compatibility issue in software integration is version mismatch, where different components or modules of integrated systems are designed to work with specific versions of underlying libraries, frameworks, or dependencies. When incompatible versions are used, it can lead to errors, crashes, or unexpected behavior, jeopardizing the stability and performance of the integrated solution. Resolving version compatibility issues often involves updating or aligning the versions of software components to ensure consistency and compatibility across the entire integration stack. This may require upgrading or downgrading libraries, frameworks, or dependencies to compatible versions, or implementing compatibility layers or shims to bridge the gap between incompatible versions. Additionally, organizations may need to refactor or modify existing code to accommodate changes in APIs, interfaces, or behavior introduced by new versions of software components. Another common compatibility challenge in software integration is platform dependency, where integrated systems rely on specific hardware, operating systems, or runtime environments that are not available or compatible with other components in the ecosystem. Platform dependency issues can arise when integrating legacy systems with modern cloud-based platforms, proprietary software with open-source solutions, or on-*

premises applications with cloud-native architectures. To resolve platform dependency issues, organizations may need to refactor or modernize legacy systems to make them compatible with modern platforms or implement compatibility layers, such as virtualization or containerization, to isolate platform-specific dependencies and ensure interoperability across heterogeneous environments. Moreover, compatibility issues can also arise due to differences in data formats, protocols, or standards used by integrated systems to exchange information or communicate with each other. For example, incompatible data formats, such as XML, JSON, or CSV, can lead to parsing errors or data loss when exchanging data between systems, while differences in communication protocols, such as HTTP, SOAP, or REST, can result in interoperability issues or communication failures. Resolving data format and protocol compatibility issues often involves implementing data transformation or mediation layers that translate between different formats or protocols, ensuring seamless data exchange and communication between integrated systems. Additionally, organizations may need to establish data governance policies and standards to ensure consistency, quality, and integrity of data exchanged between systems, reducing the risk of compatibility issues caused by data inconsistencies or discrepancies. Furthermore, resolving compatibility issues in software integration requires comprehensive testing and validation to verify that integrated systems function as expected and meet performance, reliability, and security requirements. Testing strategies may include unit testing, integration testing, regression testing, and acceptance testing to identify and address compatibility issues at different stages of the integration lifecycle. Additionally, organizations may leverage automated testing tools and frameworks to streamline testing processes, accelerate feedback cycles, and ensure robustness and reliability of integrated solutions. Moreover, organizations should consider implementing continuous integration and continuous deployment (CI/CD) pipelines to automate the deployment and validation of integration changes, enabling rapid iteration, feedback, and remediation of compatibility issues in a controlled and repeatable manner. In summary, resolving compatibility issues in software integration is essential for ensuring the seamless operation and interoperability of integrated systems within an organization's IT ecosystem. By identifying compatibility challenges, implementing targeted solutions, and testing rigorously, organizations can mitigate the risk of compatibility issues and unlock the full potential of their integrated solutions to drive innovation, efficiency, and competitiveness.

Advanced cyber threat analysis is a critical component of modern cybersecurity operations, aimed at identifying, understanding, and mitigating sophisticated cyber threats that pose significant risks to organizations' data, systems, and operations. In today's increasingly interconnected and digitized world, cyber threats are evolving rapidly in terms of complexity, sophistication, and impact, making traditional security measures insufficient to defend against them effectively. Advanced cyber threat analysis goes beyond basic threat detection and response to provide organizations with deeper insights into the tactics, techniques, and procedures (TTPs) employed by adversaries, enabling proactive threat hunting, incident response, and threat intelligence sharing. One of the key aspects of advanced cyber threat analysis is understanding the tactics, techniques, and procedures (TTPs) used by threat actors to infiltrate, exploit, and exfiltrate data from targeted systems and networks. Threat actors employ a wide range of tactics, such as phishing, malware propagation, exploitation of vulnerabilities, and social engineering, to breach defenses and gain unauthorized access to sensitive information. By studying and analyzing these TTPs, cybersecurity analysts can develop behavioral and signature-based detection methods to identify and mitigate cyber threats effectively. Moreover, advanced cyber threat analysis involves leveraging threat intelligence from various internal and external sources, such as security vendors, industry groups, government agencies, and open-source intelligence (OSINT) sources, to enrich the understanding of emerging threats, vulnerabilities, and attack trends. Threat intelligence provides valuable context and insights into the motivations, capabilities, and tactics of threat actors, enabling organizations to anticipate and proactively defend against potential cyber attacks. Additionally, advanced cyber threat analysis encompasses the use of advanced analytics and machine learning techniques to detect and respond to cyber threats in real-time. Machine learning algorithms can analyze vast amounts of security data, including network traffic, log files, and endpoint telemetry, to identify anomalous behavior patterns indicative of cyber threats, such as zero-day exploits, insider threats, or advanced persistent threats (APTs). By employing machine learning models for threat detection and classification, organizations can augment human analysts' capabilities, reduce false positives, and respond more quickly to emerging cyber threats. Furthermore, advanced cyber threat analysis involves conducting in-depth forensic investigations to understand the scope, impact, and attribution of cyber attacks. Forensic analysis techniques, such as disk imaging, memory forensics, network packet capture, and timeline analysis, enable cybersecurity analysts to reconstruct the sequence of events leading up to and following a cyber intrusion, identify compromised systems, and collect evidence for legal or regulatory purposes. Moreover, advanced cyber threat analysis includes proactive threat hunting activities aimed at identifying and mitigating potential threats before they manifest into full-blown security incidents. Threat hunting involves leveraging threat intelligence, security analytics, and human expertise to proactively search for indicators of compromise (IOCs), anomalous behavior, or signs of unauthorized access within an organization's IT environment. By adopting a proactive threat hunting mindset, organizations can detect and neutralize threats early in the attack lifecycle, reducing the likelihood of data breaches and minimizing the impact on business operations. Additionally, advanced cyber threat analysis involves continuous monitoring and assessment of cybersecurity posture to identify gaps, weaknesses, and areas for improvement in an organization's security defenses. Security assessments, such as penetration testing, vulnerability scanning, and red team exercises, enable organizations to simulate real-world cyber attacks, identify vulnerabilities, and evaluate the effectiveness of security controls in detecting and responding to threats. By conducting regular security assessments, organizations can identify and remediate security vulnerabilities proactively, strengthen their security posture, and reduce the risk of successful cyber attacks. Furthermore, advanced cyber threat analysis encompasses incident response planning and execution to ensure a coordinated and effective response to security incidents when they occur. Incident response plans define roles, responsibilities, and procedures for detecting, assessing, containing, and mitigating security incidents, enabling organizations to minimize the impact of cyber attacks and restore normal operations quickly. By establishing incident response processes and protocols in advance, organizations can respond more effectively to security incidents, mitigate potential damages, and protect their assets, reputation, and stakeholders' trust. In summary, advanced cyber threat analysis is essential for organizations to stay ahead of evolving cyber threats and protect their digital assets and operations effectively. By understanding threat actors' TTPs, leveraging threat intelligence, employing advanced analytics and machine learning, conducting forensic investigations and threat hunting, continuously monitoring cybersecurity posture, and implementing incident response capabilities, organizations can enhance their resilience to cyber threats and maintain a robust security posture in today's complex threat landscape.

Incident response planning and execution are vital components of any organization's cybersecurity strategy, aimed at effectively detecting, containing, and mitigating security incidents to minimize their impact on business operations, data integrity, and reputation. In today's cyber threat landscape, where organizations face a constant barrage of sophisticated cyber attacks and data breaches, having a well-defined incident response plan and the ability to execute it promptly and efficiently is essential for mitigating risks and ensuring business continuity. Incident response planning begins with assessing the organization's assets, risks, and vulnerabilities to identify potential security threats and determine the appropriate level of preparedness and response capabilities needed to address them. This involves conducting risk assessments, threat modeling, and gap analyses to identify critical assets, assess their value and sensitivity, and evaluate the likelihood and potential impact of security incidents on business operations. Based on the findings of the risk assessment, organizations can develop a comprehensive incident response plan that outlines roles, responsibilities, procedures, and communication channels for responding to security incidents effectively. The incident response plan should define the organization's incident response team structure, including key stakeholders, decision-makers, and subject matter experts responsible for coordinating and executing the incident response process. Moreover, the incident response plan should establish clear escalation paths and communication protocols for reporting and escalating security incidents to senior management, legal counsel, regulatory authorities, and other relevant stakeholders as necessary. This ensures that incidents are promptly and effectively communicated to the appropriate stakeholders, enabling timely decision-making and response coordination. Additionally, the incident response plan should define the procedures and processes for incident detection, classification, and prioritization to ensure a systematic and consistent approach to incident handling. This includes establishing criteria for classifying incidents based on severity, impact, and urgency, as well as defining response priorities and escalation thresholds for different types of incidents. By categorizing incidents according to their severity and impact, organizations can prioritize response efforts and allocate resources effectively to mitigate the most critical threats first. Furthermore, the incident response plan should outline the technical and operational procedures for incident containment, eradication, and recovery to minimize the duration and impact of security incidents on business operations. This includes defining procedures for isolating affected systems, containing the spread of malware or malicious activity, and restoring affected services and data to their pre-incident state. Additionally, organizations should establish incident response playbooks or runbooks that provide step-by-step instructions and guidelines for responding to specific types of security incidents, such as malware infections, data breaches, or denial-of-service attacks. These playbooks should include predefined response actions, decision trees, and checklists to guide incident responders through the incident response process systematically. Moreover, incident response planning should include regular training, testing, and exercises to ensure that the incident response team is prepared to execute the incident response plan effectively in a real-world scenario. This involves conducting tabletop exercises, simulation drills, and red team exercises to simulate different types of security incidents and evaluate the organization's response capabilities, communication processes, and coordination efforts. By regularly testing and refining the incident response plan through training and exercises, organizations can identify weaknesses, gaps, and areas for improvement in their incident response capabilities and make necessary adjustments to enhance their readiness and resilience to cyber threats. Additionally, incident response planning should include post-incident activities, such as lessons learned sessions, root cause analysis, and process improvements, to identify opportunities for enhancing incident response effectiveness and preventing future incidents. This involves conducting thorough post-incident reviews to analyze the organization's response to the incident, identify areas for improvement, and implement corrective actions and preventive measures to mitigate similar incidents in the future. By capturing lessons learned from past incidents and incorporating them into the incident response plan, organizations can continuously improve their incident response capabilities and strengthen their overall security posture. In summary, incident response planning and execution are critical components of effective cybersecurity management, enabling organizations to detect, contain, and mitigate security incidents promptly and efficiently. By developing a comprehensive incident response plan, defining clear roles and responsibilities, establishing communication protocols, and conducting regular training and exercises, organizations can enhance their readiness and resilience to cyber threats and minimize the impact of security incidents on their business operations, data assets, and reputation.

Data center performance optimization is a multifaceted process aimed at maximizing the efficiency, reliability, and scalability of data center infrastructure to meet the growing demands of modern digital businesses. In today's hyperconnected world, where organizations rely heavily on data-intensive applications, cloud services, and digital platforms to drive innovation, collaboration, and competitiveness, ensuring optimal performance of data center operations is crucial for delivering a seamless and responsive user experience, minimizing downtime, and optimizing resource utilization. The optimization of data center performance begins with a comprehensive assessment of the existing infrastructure, including servers, storage, networking, and cooling systems, to identify potential bottlenecks, inefficiencies, and areas for improvement. This involves analyzing key performance indicators (KPIs) such as server utilization, network latency, storage throughput, and power consumption to gain insights into the overall health and performance of the data center environment. By identifying performance bottlenecks and areas of resource contention, organizations can develop targeted strategies and solutions to address them effectively and optimize data center performance. One of the key strategies for optimizing data center performance is server consolidation and virtualization, which involves consolidating multiple physical servers onto a smaller number of virtualized servers to improve resource utilization, reduce hardware costs, and increase flexibility and scalability. Virtualization enables organizations to allocate and reallocate computing resources dynamically based on workload demand, optimizing server utilization and improving overall data center efficiency. Moreover, server virtualization enables organizations to implement advanced features such as live migration, high availability, and workload balancing, which further enhance the resilience, agility, and scalability of data center operations. Another important aspect of data center performance optimization is network optimization, which involves optimizing network architecture, configuration, and protocols to improve network performance, reliability, and security. This includes implementing technologies such as quality of service (QoS), traffic shaping, and network segmentation to prioritize critical traffic, minimize latency, and ensure optimal network performance for mission-critical applications and services. Additionally, organizations can leverage software-defined networking (SDN) and network function virtualization (NFV) to automate network provisioning, optimize traffic flows, and improve network agility and scalability. Furthermore, data center performance optimization involves optimizing storage infrastructure to improve storage efficiency, performance, and reliability while reducing costs and complexity. This includes implementing storage tiering, deduplication, compression, and thin provisioning techniques to optimize storage utilization and reduce storage footprint. Additionally, organizations can leverage technologies such as flash storage, software-defined storage (SDS), and hyper-converged infrastructure (HCI) to accelerate storage performance, simplify management, and improve scalability and flexibility. Moreover, data center performance optimization encompasses optimizing cooling and power management to improve energy efficiency, reduce operating costs, and minimize environmental impact. This includes implementing energy-efficient cooling systems, optimizing airflow management, and deploying power management technologies such as dynamic voltage and frequency scaling (DVFS) and power capping to reduce energy consumption and heat generation. Additionally, organizations can leverage data center infrastructure management (DCIM) solutions to monitor and optimize power usage, cooling efficiency, and overall energy consumption in real-time, enabling proactive management and optimization of data center resources. Furthermore, data center performance optimization involves implementing proactive monitoring, analytics, and automation tools to continuously monitor, analyze, and optimize data center performance in real-time. This includes deploying performance monitoring tools, log management systems, and predictive analytics solutions to identify performance anomalies, predict potential issues, and proactively address them before they impact business operations. Additionally, organizations can leverage automation and orchestration tools to automate routine tasks, streamline operations, and improve efficiency, allowing IT teams to focus on more strategic initiatives and innovation. Moreover, data center performance optimization requires adopting a holistic and lifecycle approach to data center design, deployment, and management, taking into account factors such as capacity planning, workload optimization, and lifecycle management. This includes designing data center infrastructure with scalability, flexibility, and resilience in mind, to accommodate future growth and evolving business requirements. Additionally, organizations should regularly review and update their data center performance optimization strategies and solutions to keep pace with technological advancements, changing business needs, and evolving regulatory requirements. By continuously optimizing data center performance, organizations can improve agility, reduce costs, enhance user experience, and gain a competitive edge in today's digital economy.

Troubleshooting hardware and software issues in data centers is a critical aspect of maintaining optimal performance, reliability, and availability of IT infrastructure. In the dynamic and complex environment of modern data centers, hardware and software problems can arise due to various factors, including hardware failures, software bugs, configuration errors, and compatibility issues. Effectively identifying, diagnosing, and resolving these issues is essential to minimize downtime, prevent data loss, and ensure seamless operations. When troubleshooting hardware issues in data centers, it's crucial to start by gathering relevant information about the affected hardware components, such as server models, specifications, and configurations. This information helps in understanding the hardware architecture, identifying potential points of failure, and determining the scope of the problem. Common hardware issues in data centers include hardware failures, such as server crashes, disk failures, memory errors, and network card issues. Troubleshooting hardware failures often involves performing diagnostic tests, such as hardware diagnostics, system logs analysis, and physical inspection of hardware components, to identify the root cause of the problem. Additionally, organizations can leverage hardware monitoring and management tools to monitor the health and performance of hardware components in real-time, detect anomalies, and proactively address potential hardware issues before they escalate into critical failures. Furthermore, when troubleshooting software issues in data centers, it's essential to start by identifying the affected software applications, services, or operating systems and gathering relevant information about their configurations, dependencies, and usage patterns. Common software issues in data centers include software bugs, configuration errors, compatibility issues, and performance bottlenecks. Troubleshooting software issues often involves analyzing system logs, error messages, and performance metrics to identify the root cause of the problem. Additionally, organizations can leverage software debugging tools, log analysis tools, and performance monitoring solutions to diagnose software issues, pinpoint performance bottlenecks, and optimize software configurations for improved performance and reliability. Moreover, when troubleshooting hardware and software issues in data centers, it's essential to follow a systematic approach to problem-solving, starting with basic troubleshooting steps and progressively narrowing down the possible causes of the problem. This involves gathering information about the symptoms, performing diagnostic tests, isolating the problem, and implementing targeted solutions to resolve the issue. Additionally, organizations can leverage troubleshooting methodologies, such as root cause analysis (RCA), fault tree analysis (FTA), and fishbone diagrams, to systematically identify and address the underlying causes of hardware and software issues in data centers. Furthermore, effective communication and collaboration are essential when troubleshooting hardware and software issues in data centers, as it often requires the involvement of multiple teams, including IT operations, network engineering, system administrators, and application developers. Clear and timely communication helps in coordinating troubleshooting efforts, sharing information, and aligning stakeholders' expectations to ensure a prompt and effective resolution of the problem. Additionally, organizations can establish incident response processes and escalation procedures to streamline communication and coordination during troubleshooting activities, enabling quick decision-making and problem resolution. Moreover, documentation plays a crucial role in troubleshooting hardware and software issues in data centers, as it provides a record of past incidents, solutions, and best practices for future reference. Organizations should maintain up-to-date documentation of hardware and software configurations, troubleshooting procedures, known issues, and resolutions to facilitate efficient problem-solving and knowledge sharing among IT teams.

Additionally, organizations can leverage knowledge management systems, wikis, and collaboration platforms to capture and share troubleshooting knowledge and expertise across the organization. Furthermore, proactive maintenance and preventive measures are essential for minimizing hardware and software issues in data centers and ensuring ongoing reliability and performance. This includes regular hardware maintenance, firmware updates, software patches, and security updates to address known vulnerabilities and mitigate potential risks. Additionally, organizations can implement monitoring and alerting systems to proactively detect and respond to hardware and software issues before they impact business operations. By continuously monitoring hardware and software health, performance, and security, organizations can identify potential issues early, take proactive measures to address them, and prevent costly downtime and data loss. In summary, troubleshooting hardware and software issues in data centers requires a systematic approach, effective communication, collaboration, documentation, and proactive maintenance. By following best practices and leveraging the right tools and methodologies, organizations can minimize downtime, improve reliability, and ensure the seamless operation of data center infrastructure in today's dynamic and demanding IT environments.

Troubleshooting cloud service outages is a critical aspect of managing cloud infrastructure and ensuring the availability, reliability, and performance of cloud-based services. In today's digital era, where businesses rely heavily on cloud computing for their IT operations, any disruption in cloud services can have significant implications for business continuity, customer satisfaction, and revenue generation. Therefore, effective troubleshooting of cloud service outages is essential to minimize downtime, restore service functionality, and mitigate the impact on users and stakeholders. Cloud service outages can occur due to various factors, including infrastructure failures, network issues, software bugs, configuration errors, and cyber attacks. When troubleshooting cloud service outages, it's essential to start by gathering relevant information about the affected services, such as service status, error messages, performance metrics, and user reports. This information helps in understanding the scope and severity of the outage, identifying potential points of failure, and determining the appropriate course of action for troubleshooting and resolution. Common causes of cloud service outages include hardware failures, such as server crashes, storage failures, and network outages, which can disrupt service availability and performance. Troubleshooting hardware-related outages often involves performing diagnostic tests, hardware diagnostics, and physical inspection of hardware components to identify the root cause of the problem and implement corrective actions to restore service functionality. Additionally, organizations can leverage infrastructure monitoring and management tools to monitor the health and performance of cloud infrastructure in real-time, detect hardware failures, and proactively address potential issues before they escalate into service outages. Furthermore, network issues, such as network congestion, routing errors, and DDoS attacks, can also cause cloud service outages by disrupting communication between cloud servers and client devices. Troubleshooting network-related outages requires analyzing network traffic, logs, and performance metrics to identify anomalies and potential points of failure in the network infrastructure. Additionally, organizations can leverage network monitoring and security solutions to monitor network traffic, detect and mitigate DDoS attacks, and ensure the availability and reliability of network connectivity for cloud services. Moreover, software bugs, configuration errors, and compatibility issues can also cause cloud service outages by impacting the functionality, performance, or stability of cloud-based applications and services. Troubleshooting software-related outages often involves analyzing application logs, error messages, and performance metrics to identify the root cause of the problem and implement corrective actions, such as software patches, configuration changes, or rollback procedures, to restore service functionality.

Additionally, organizations can leverage application performance monitoring (APM) solutions to monitor the performance and availability of cloud-based applications, identify performance bottlenecks, and optimize application configurations for improved reliability and performance. Furthermore, cyber attacks, such as DDoS attacks, ransomware attacks, and data breaches, can also cause cloud service outages by disrupting service availability, compromising data integrity, or causing service degradation. Troubleshooting security-related outages requires analyzing security logs, intrusion detection alerts, and forensic evidence to identify the nature and scope of the attack and implement appropriate countermeasures to mitigate the impact and prevent future attacks. Additionally, organizations can leverage security information and event management (SIEM) solutions, threat intelligence feeds, and security incident response procedures to detect, analyze, and respond to security incidents in real-time, minimizing the impact on cloud services and data assets. Moreover, when troubleshooting cloud service outages, it's essential to follow a systematic approach to problem-solving, starting with basic troubleshooting steps and progressively narrowing down the possible causes of the problem. This involves gathering information about the symptoms, performing diagnostic tests, isolating the problem, and implementing targeted solutions to restore service functionality. Additionally, organizations can leverage incident response processes, escalation procedures, and communication protocols to streamline *troubleshooting efforts, coordinate response activities, and keep stakeholders informed about the status and progress of the outage resolution. Furthermore, proactive monitoring, maintenance, and preventive measures are essential for minimizing cloud service outages and ensuring ongoing reliability, availability, and performance of cloud-based services. This includes implementing robust monitoring and alerting systems, conducting regular maintenance activities, such as software updates, security patches, and hardware upgrades, and implementing disaster recovery and business continuity plans to mitigate the impact of potential outages on business operations. By following best practices and leveraging the right tools and methodologies, organizations can effectively troubleshoot cloud service outages, minimize downtime, and ensure the seamless operation of cloud-based services in today's dynamic and demanding IT environments.*

Cloud security and compliance challenges represent significant hurdles for organizations migrating their IT infrastructure and data to cloud environments. As businesses increasingly rely on cloud services for storage, processing, and hosting sensitive information, ensuring the security and compliance of these environments becomes paramount. However, navigating the complex landscape of cloud security and compliance can be daunting due to the unique risks and regulatory requirements associated with cloud computing. One of the primary challenges in cloud security is data protection. When data is stored and processed in the cloud, it becomes susceptible to various security threats, such as unauthorized access, data breaches, and data loss. Ensuring the confidentiality, integrity, and availability of data in the cloud requires robust encryption, access controls, and data loss prevention measures. Additionally, organizations must implement secure authentication and authorization mechanisms to control access to cloud resources and ensure that only authorized users can access sensitive data and applications. Another significant challenge in cloud security is network security. With cloud services being accessed over the internet, securing network connections and data transmissions becomes critical to prevent eavesdropping, man-in-the-middle attacks, and other network-based threats. Implementing secure network protocols, such as SSL/TLS encryption and VPN tunnels, can help protect data in transit and mitigate the risk of network-based attacks. Moreover, organizations must implement network segmentation and firewall rules to isolate cloud resources and prevent unauthorized access between different parts of the cloud environment. Additionally, ensuring the security and compliance of cloud infrastructure requires robust identity and access management (IAM) practices. IAM controls and monitors user access to cloud resources, ensuring that only authorized users and devices can access sensitive data and applications. Implementing strong authentication mechanisms, such as multi-factor authentication (MFA) and biometric authentication, can help verify the identity of users and prevent unauthorized access to cloud services. Furthermore, *organizations must regularly review and update access permissions and roles to ensure that they align with business requirements and security policies. Compliance with regulatory requirements is another significant challenge in cloud security. Many industries are subject to strict regulations governing the protection and privacy of sensitive data, such as healthcare data (HIPAA), financial data (PCI DSS), and personal data (GDPR). Ensuring compliance with these regulations when using cloud services requires organizations to implement robust security controls, data encryption, and audit trails to demonstrate compliance with regulatory requirements. Additionally, organizations must carefully select cloud service providers that offer compliance certifications and adhere to industry best practices for data security and privacy. Furthermore, ensuring cloud security and compliance requires ongoing monitoring, auditing, and risk assessment. Organizations must continuously monitor cloud environments for security incidents, anomalous activities, and compliance violations, using security information and event management (SIEM) systems, intrusion detection systems (IDS), and log management solutions. Additionally, organizations must conduct regular security audits and assessments to identify vulnerabilities, assess risks, and implement remediation measures to strengthen cloud security posture and ensure compliance with regulatory requirements. Moreover, organizations must stay informed about emerging threats, security vulnerabilities, and regulatory changes that may impact cloud security and compliance. This requires continuous education, training, and collaboration among IT teams, security professionals, and compliance officers to stay abreast of the latest developments in cloud security and compliance and adapt their strategies and practices accordingly. In summary, cloud security and compliance challenges pose significant risks and complexities for organizations leveraging cloud services. By implementing robust security controls, access management practices, and compliance measures, organizations can mitigate these risks and ensure the security, integrity, and compliance of their data and applications in the cloud. However, addressing these challenges requires a holistic approach, ongoing vigilance, and collaboration across the organization to effectively protect sensitive information and maintain regulatory compliance in today's dynamic and evolving cloud environment.*

IoT (Internet of Things) devices have become increasingly prevalent in various sectors, including healthcare, manufacturing, transportation, and smart homes, enabling the collection of vast amounts of data and the automation of processes. However, ensuring the optimal performance of IoT devices poses unique challenges due to their distributed nature, diverse configurations, and resource constraints. Effective IoT device performance monitoring is essential to identify potential issues, optimize device functionality, and maintain the reliability and efficiency of IoT deployments. One of the primary challenges in IoT device performance monitoring is the sheer scale and diversity of IoT deployments. With thousands or even millions of IoT devices deployed across different locations and environments, monitoring and managing their performance can be a daunting task. Organizations must implement scalable and centralized monitoring solutions that can collect, analyze, and visualize data from a wide range of IoT devices, sensors, and gateways in real-time. Additionally, organizations must consider the heterogeneity of IoT devices, which may vary in terms of hardware specifications, communication protocols, and software configurations. Monitoring solutions must be able to support diverse device types and protocols, such as MQTT, CoAP, and HTTP, and provide standardized interfaces for data integration and analysis. Moreover, IoT devices often operate in resource-constrained environments with limited processing power, memory, and bandwidth. Monitoring solutions must be lightweight and efficient, consuming minimal system resources and network bandwidth to avoid impacting device performance. This requires the use of optimized data collection methods, such as edge computing and data aggregation, to reduce the overhead of monitoring and ensure minimal impact on device operations. Furthermore, IoT devices are often deployed in harsh or remote environments, such as industrial facilities, outdoor settings, and vehicles, where environmental factors, such as temperature, humidity, and vibration, can affect device performance. Monitoring solutions must be able to withstand these environmental conditions and provide reliable operation in challenging deployment scenarios. This may require the use of ruggedized hardware, wireless connectivity options, and battery backup systems to ensure continuous monitoring and data collection in adverse conditions. Additionally, IoT devices may be susceptible to various performance issues, such as hardware failures, software bugs, network connectivity issues, and sensor drift. Monitoring solutions must be able to detect these issues in real-time and provide alerts and notifications to administrators and operators to facilitate timely intervention and troubleshooting. This requires the use of anomaly detection algorithms, predictive analytics, and machine learning techniques to identify deviations from normal device behavior and predict potential issues before they impact operations.

Moreover, IoT deployments often involve complex ecosystems of interconnected devices, sensors, gateways, and cloud services, making it challenging to trace performance issues across the entire IoT infrastructure. Monitoring solutions must provide end-to-end visibility into the performance of the entire IoT ecosystem, from device endpoints to cloud backends, to identify bottlenecks, optimize data flows, and ensure seamless operation. This requires the integration of monitoring data from multiple sources, such as device telemetry, network traffic, and application logs, into a unified dashboard or analytics platform for comprehensive performance analysis and troubleshooting. Additionally, IoT device performance monitoring must address the unique security and privacy challenges associated with IoT deployments. With the proliferation of IoT devices, the attack surface for cyber threats has expanded, making IoT devices attractive targets for hackers and malicious actors. Monitoring solutions must implement robust security measures, such as data encryption, access controls, and intrusion detection, to protect sensitive IoT data and prevent unauthorized access to devices and networks. Moreover, IoT device performance monitoring must comply with data privacy regulations, such as GDPR and CCPA, which impose strict requirements on the collection, processing, and storage of personal data generated by IoT devices. Organizations must implement privacy-by-design principles and anonymization techniques to ensure the privacy and confidentiality of IoT data while still enabling effective performance monitoring and analysis. Furthermore, IoT device performance monitoring must support scalability and flexibility to accommodate the dynamic nature of IoT deployments and evolving business requirements. As IoT deployments grow in scale and complexity, monitoring solutions must be able to scale seamlessly to handle increasing data volumes, device counts, and user demands. This requires the use of cloud-based monitoring platforms, microservices architectures, and containerization techniques to enable elastic scaling and on-demand provisioning of monitoring resources. Additionally, monitoring solutions must be flexible and adaptable to support different deployment models, such as on-premises, hybrid, and multi-cloud environments, and integrate with existing IT infrastructure and toolsets. In summary, IoT device performance monitoring is essential for ensuring the reliability, efficiency, and security of IoT deployments. By implementing scalable, efficient, and robust monitoring solutions, organizations can proactively identify and address performance issues, optimize device operations, and maximize the value of their IoT investments. However, addressing the unique challenges of IoT device performance monitoring requires a holistic approach, combining technical expertise, best practices, and innovative technologies to meet the evolving needs of IoT deployments in today's digital age. Resolving connectivity issues in IoT (Internet of Things) networks is crucial for maintaining the functionality, reliability, and performance of IoT deployments. With the proliferation of IoT devices and the growing complexity of IoT ecosystems, connectivity issues can arise due to various factors, including network congestion, signal interference, device malfunction, and configuration errors. Effectively resolving these issues requires a systematic approach, involving troubleshooting techniques, diagnostic tools, and proactive measures to identify and address the root causes of connectivity problems. One of the most common causes of connectivity issues in IoT networks is network congestion, which occurs when the network bandwidth is insufficient to accommodate the volume of data generated by IoT devices. This can lead to delays, packet loss, and degraded performance, affecting the responsiveness and reliability of IoT applications. Resolving network congestion requires optimizing network traffic, prioritizing critical data flows, and implementing Quality of Service (QoS) policies to ensure timely delivery of important data packets. Additionally, organizations can deploy edge computing solutions to process data closer to the source, reducing the burden on the network and improving overall network performance. Another common cause of connectivity issues in IoT networks is signal interference, which occurs when multiple wireless devices operate in the same frequency band, causing signal collisions and disruptions. Signal interference can be caused by nearby electronic devices, physical obstacles, or environmental factors, such as electromagnetic interference (EMI) and radio frequency (RF) noise. Resolving signal interference requires identifying the sources of interference and taking corrective actions, such as relocating devices, adjusting transmission power levels, or using alternative frequency bands. Additionally, organizations can deploy mesh networking protocols, such as Zigbee or Thread, which can dynamically reroute traffic and optimize communication paths to avoid interference and improve network reliability. Moreover, device malfunction can also contribute to connectivity issues in IoT networks, as faulty hardware or software can prevent devices from communicating effectively with the network or other devices. Resolving device malfunction requires diagnosing the root cause of the problem and implementing remediation measures, such as firmware updates, hardware replacements, or configuration adjustments. Additionally, organizations can deploy remote device management platforms that provide real-time monitoring, troubleshooting, and maintenance capabilities to identify and address device issues proactively. Furthermore, configuration errors can lead to connectivity issues in IoT networks, as misconfigured devices or network settings can cause communication failures or security vulnerabilities. Resolving configuration errors requires reviewing and validating device configurations, ensuring consistency and compliance with network policies and best practices. Additionally, organizations can implement configuration management tools and automation solutions to streamline device provisioning, deployment, and maintenance processes, reducing the risk of human error and ensuring the integrity of device configurations. Additionally, organizations can leverage network monitoring and management tools to monitor the performance and availability of IoT devices and identify connectivity issues proactively. These tools provide real-time visibility into network traffic, device status, and performance metrics, enabling administrators to detect anomalies, troubleshoot problems, and implement corrective actions before they impact operations. Moreover, organizations can implement redundancy and failover mechanisms to ensure high availability and fault tolerance in IoT networks. By deploying redundant network links, backup servers, and failover clusters, organizations can minimize the impact of connectivity issues and maintain continuity of operations in the event of network failures or disruptions. Additionally, organizations can implement load balancing and traffic shaping techniques to distribute network traffic evenly across multiple paths and optimize resource utilization, improving overall network performance and reliability. Furthermore, organizations can implement security measures to protect IoT networks from cyber threats and attacks, such as unauthorized access, data breaches, and malware infections. By implementing network segmentation, access controls, encryption, and intrusion detection systems (IDS), organizations can prevent unauthorized access to IoT devices and data, detect suspicious activities, and respond to security incidents in a timely manner. Additionally, organizations can educate users and employees about cybersecurity best practices, such as strong password management, software updates, and phishing awareness, to mitigate the risk of security breaches and protect sensitive information. In summary, resolving connectivity issues in

IoT networks requires a proactive and multifaceted approach, involving troubleshooting techniques, diagnostic tools, and proactive measures to identify and address the root causes of connectivity problems. By implementing best practices, optimizing network infrastructure, and implementing security measures, organizations can ensure the reliability, performance, and security of their IoT deployments in today's digital age.

Implementing machine learning models for predictive maintenance represents a paradigm shift in how organizations manage their assets, optimize maintenance schedules, and reduce downtime. Predictive maintenance leverages advanced analytics and machine learning algorithms to predict equipment failures before they occur, allowing organizations to schedule maintenance activities proactively and avoid costly unplanned downtime. By analyzing historical data, sensor readings, and equipment telemetry, machine learning models can identify patterns, trends, and anomalies indicative of impending failures or degradation in equipment performance. This enables organizations to anticipate maintenance needs, prioritize resources, and optimize maintenance schedules to maximize asset reliability and availability. One of the key benefits of implementing machine learning models for predictive maintenance is the ability to transition from reactive or scheduled maintenance approaches to a more proactive and data-driven maintenance strategy. Instead of waiting for equipment to fail or adhering to rigid maintenance schedules, organizations can use predictive maintenance to monitor equipment health in real-time, detect early warning signs of potential failures, and take preemptive action to address issues before they escalate. This shift from reactive to proactive maintenance can significantly reduce downtime, improve asset uptime, and extend the lifespan of equipment, resulting in cost savings and operational efficiencies. Moreover, predictive maintenance enables organizations to move away from one-size-fits-all maintenance schedules to more targeted and optimized maintenance plans tailored to the specific needs and usage patterns of each asset. Machine learning models can analyze historical maintenance data, equipment performance metrics, and environmental factors to develop predictive maintenance algorithms that take into account the unique characteristics and operating conditions of each asset. This allows organizations to schedule maintenance activities based on actual equipment condition, usage patterns, and performance degradation trends, rather than arbitrary time-based intervals or fixed schedules. Additionally, machine learning models can continuously learn and adapt to changing operating conditions, equipment behavior, and environmental factors, allowing organizations to refine and improve their predictive maintenance strategies over time. This iterative approach to predictive maintenance enables organizations to achieve higher levels of accuracy, reliability, and effectiveness in predicting equipment failures and optimizing maintenance schedules. Furthermore, implementing machine learning models for predictive maintenance enables organizations to harness the power of big data and advanced analytics to extract actionable insights from vast amounts of data generated by IoT sensors, equipment telemetry, and maintenance records. By integrating data from disparate sources, such as equipment sensors, maintenance logs, and enterprise systems, machine learning models can identify hidden patterns, correlations, and relationships that traditional maintenance approaches may overlook. This holistic view of equipment health and performance enables organizations to make informed decisions, prioritize maintenance activities, and allocate resources more effectively to maximize asset uptime and minimize maintenance costs. Additionally, machine learning models can help organizations identify early warning signs of potential equipment failures or degradation that may not be apparent to human operators or traditional maintenance systems. By analyzing sensor data, equipment telemetry, and historical maintenance records, machine learning models can detect subtle changes in equipment behavior, performance metrics, or environmental conditions that may indicate impending failures or degradation in equipment health. This early detection capability allows organizations to take proactive measures to address issues before they escalate into costly failures, minimizing downtime, and avoiding potential safety hazards or production losses. Moreover, implementing machine learning models for predictive maintenance can enable organizations to transition from reactive to prescriptive maintenance approaches, where maintenance actions are not only predicted but also optimized to achieve specific business objectives, such as maximizing equipment uptime, minimizing maintenance costs, or optimizing asset performance. By integrating machine learning models with optimization algorithms, organizations can develop prescriptive maintenance strategies that consider various factors, such as equipment criticality, business priorities, resource constraints, and regulatory requirements, to recommend the most cost-effective and efficient maintenance actions to achieve desired outcomes. This data-driven approach to maintenance decision-making enables organizations to optimize their maintenance workflows, allocate resources more effectively, and achieve higher levels of asset reliability, availability, and performance. In summary, implementing machine learning models for predictive maintenance offers organizations a powerful tool for optimizing maintenance schedules, reducing downtime, and maximizing asset reliability and availability. By leveraging advanced analytics, big data, and machine learning algorithms, organizations can transition from reactive to proactive maintenance strategies, develop targeted and optimized maintenance plans, and achieve higher levels of accuracy, efficiency, and effectiveness in predicting equipment failures and optimizing maintenance schedules. However, successful implementation of predictive maintenance requires careful consideration of data quality, model accuracy, scalability, and organizational readiness to ensure that machine learning models deliver actionable insights and tangible business value in real-world operational environments.

Using AI for proactive troubleshooting revolutionizes how organizations address technical issues, predict potential failures, and maintain operational continuity. It entails harnessing the power of artificial intelligence algorithms and machine learning techniques to analyze vast amounts of data, detect anomalies, and anticipate problems before they occur. By leveraging historical data, real-time telemetry, and predictive analytics, AI-driven systems can identify patterns, trends, and deviations indicative of impending issues or degradation in system performance. This proactive approach enables organizations to take preemptive action, mitigate risks, and prevent costly downtime or service disruptions. One of the primary benefits of using AI for proactive troubleshooting is the ability to shift from reactive firefighting to a proactive and preventative maintenance mindset. Instead of waiting for problems to manifest and then scrambling to resolve them, organizations can use AI-powered systems to continuously monitor system health, detect early warning signs of potential issues, and initiate corrective actions proactively. This proactive stance helps organizations avoid the productivity losses, service disruptions, and reputational damage associated with reactive troubleshooting, leading to improved operational efficiency and customer satisfaction. Moreover, AI-driven proactive troubleshooting enables organizations to identify and address underlying root causes of recurring issues, rather than merely treating symptoms. By analyzing historical incident data, correlating events, and identifying common patterns, AI algorithms can uncover systemic issues, software bugs, or configuration errors that contribute to repeated failures or performance degradation. This deeper understanding allows organizations to implement targeted remediation measures, optimize system configurations, and improve overall system reliability and stability. Additionally, AI-powered proactive troubleshooting can help organizations optimize resource allocation and prioritize remediation efforts based on the severity, impact, and likelihood of potential issues. By analyzing historical incident data, service level agreements (SLAs), and business priorities, AI algorithms can recommend the most appropriate response actions, allocate resources efficiently, and minimize the impact of technical issues on critical business operations. This intelligent resource allocation enables organizations to optimize their incident response workflows, improve operational agility, and deliver higher levels of service reliability and availability. Furthermore, AI-driven proactive troubleshooting can enhance the scalability and resilience of IT operations by automating routine tasks, optimizing system configurations, and adapting to changing environmental conditions. By continuously learning from past incidents, analyzing emerging trends, and updating predictive models, AI systems can adapt and evolve over time, becoming more effective at identifying and resolving issues before they escalate. This adaptability and scalability enable organizations to maintain operational continuity, even in the face of growing complexity, increasing workload demands, and evolving technology landscapes. Moreover, AI-powered proactive troubleshooting can help organizations detect and mitigate security threats and vulnerabilities before they can be exploited by malicious actors. By analyzing network traffic, system logs, and user behavior patterns, AI algorithms can identify suspicious activities, anomalous behavior, and potential security breaches in real-time. This early detection capability enables organizations to take swift action, implement security controls, and prevent unauthorized access or data breaches, safeguarding sensitive information and protecting critical assets from cyber threats. Additionally, AI-driven proactive troubleshooting can help organizations improve regulatory compliance and demonstrate due diligence by maintaining comprehensive audit trails, documenting incident response actions, and providing evidence of proactive risk management practices. This proactive approach to cybersecurity enables organizations to reduce the likelihood of regulatory fines, legal liabilities, and reputational damage associated with data breaches or compliance violations. In summary, using AI for proactive troubleshooting represents a transformative shift in how organizations manage technical issues, mitigate risks, and maintain operational continuity in today's fast-paced and complex IT environments. By harnessing the power of artificial intelligence, machine learning, and predictive analytics, organizations can anticipate problems before they occur, optimize resource allocation, and enhance the reliability, security, and scalability of their IT operations. However, successful implementation of AI-powered proactive troubleshooting requires a holistic approach that integrates people, processes, and technology, fosters a culture of collaboration and continuous improvement, and aligns with strategic business objectives.

Troubleshooting challenges in blockchain technology present unique complexities and obstacles that require specialized expertise and strategies to overcome. Blockchain, a decentralized and immutable ledger technology, introduces several complexities in terms of troubleshooting due to its distributed nature, cryptographic principles, and consensus mechanisms. One of the primary challenges in troubleshooting blockchain technology is the decentralized nature of blockchain networks. Unlike traditional centralized systems where a single entity has control over the network, blockchain networks are distributed among multiple nodes, each maintaining a copy of the ledger. This decentralized architecture complicates troubleshooting efforts as issues may arise from various nodes or network segments, requiring comprehensive monitoring and analysis to identify the root cause. Additionally, blockchain networks often operate across multiple jurisdictions and geopolitical boundaries, further complicating troubleshooting efforts due to regulatory differences, legal constraints, and jurisdictional issues that may impact network operations and governance. Another significant challenge in troubleshooting blockchain technology is the complexity of cryptographic algorithms and protocols used to secure transactions and validate blocks. Blockchain relies heavily on cryptographic principles, such as hash functions, digital signatures, and consensus algorithms, to ensure data integrity, immutability, and trustlessness. However, cryptographic vulnerabilities, implementation errors, or protocol weaknesses can introduce security risks and compromise the integrity of the blockchain network. Troubleshooting cryptographic issues requires specialized knowledge of cryptography, cryptographic algorithms, and cryptographic libraries, as well as access to cryptographic experts who can analyze and address security vulnerabilities effectively. Furthermore, troubleshooting blockchain technology involves addressing performance bottlenecks and scalability limitations that may arise as blockchain networks grow in size and transaction volume. As blockchain networks scale to accommodate increased transaction throughput and user activity, they may encounter challenges related to network congestion, transaction latency, and consensus overhead. These performance issues can impact the user experience, degrade network performance, and hinder adoption and scalability. Troubleshooting performance-related issues in blockchain networks requires a deep understanding of network architecture, consensus algorithms, and scalability techniques, as well as the ability to optimize network parameters, implement performance tuning strategies, and deploy scaling solutions, such as sharding or off-chain scaling solutions. Additionally, troubleshooting blockchain technology involves addressing governance and consensus challenges that may arise from divergent interests, conflicting incentives, and governance disputes within decentralized networks. Blockchain networks often rely on consensus mechanisms, such as proof-of-work (PoW) or proof-of-stake (PoS), to achieve agreement among network participants and validate transactions. However, consensus failures, governance disputes, or protocol changes can lead to network forks, consensus disruptions, or governance crises that require careful coordination and consensus-building efforts to resolve. Troubleshooting governance and consensus issues in blockchain networks requires collaboration among network stakeholders, transparent communication channels, and robust governance mechanisms to address conflicts, reconcile differences, and maintain network integrity. Moreover, troubleshooting blockchain technology involves addressing interoperability challenges that may arise when integrating blockchain networks with existing IT systems, legacy infrastructure, or external platforms. Blockchain interoperability refers to the ability of different blockchain networks to communicate, share data, and transact seamlessly across heterogeneous environments. However, interoperability challenges, such as data format mismatches, protocol inconsistencies, or network incompatibilities, can impede data exchange, hinder collaboration, and limit the adoption of blockchain technology. Troubleshooting interoperability issues in blockchain networks requires standardization efforts, protocol enhancements, and interoperability frameworks that enable seamless integration and data exchange across disparate blockchain networks and platforms. Furthermore, troubleshooting blockchain technology involves addressing privacy and security concerns that may arise from the immutable and transparent nature of blockchain ledgers. While blockchain offers robust security features, such as cryptographic hashing, encryption, and consensus mechanisms, it also raises privacy concerns related to data confidentiality, identity protection, and regulatory compliance. Troubleshooting privacy and security issues in blockchain networks requires implementing privacy-enhancing technologies, such as zero-knowledge proofs, secure multiparty computation, and data anonymization techniques, to protect sensitive information and ensure compliance with data protection regulations, such as GDPR or HIPAA. Additionally, troubleshooting blockchain technology involves addressing regulatory and compliance challenges that may arise from evolving regulatory frameworks, legal uncertainties, and jurisdictional differences governing blockchain-based transactions and applications. Blockchain technology operates in a rapidly evolving regulatory landscape characterized by varying degrees of regulatory clarity and enforcement across different jurisdictions. Troubleshooting regulatory and compliance issues in blockchain networks requires legal expertise, regulatory awareness, and compliance frameworks that enable organizations to navigate regulatory requirements, address compliance risks, and ensure legal compliance in their blockchain initiatives. In summary, troubleshooting blockchain technology presents unique challenges and complexities that require specialized knowledge, expertise, and strategies to overcome effectively. From decentralized architectures and cryptographic principles to performance scalability and regulatory compliance, addressing troubleshooting challenges in blockchain technology requires a multidisciplinary approach that integrates technical, regulatory, and governance considerations to ensure the reliability, security, and scalability of blockchain networks in today's digital economy. Resolving issues in augmented reality (AR) and virtual reality (VR) systems requires a comprehensive understanding of the underlying technologies, hardware components, software platforms, and user experiences involved in these immersive environments. AR and VR technologies have gained significant traction in various industries, including gaming, entertainment, education, healthcare, and enterprise applications, offering immersive experiences and transformative capabilities. However, like any emerging technology, AR and VR systems encounter challenges related to hardware limitations, software compatibility, user interface design, content creation, and user experience optimization. One of the primary challenges in resolving issues in AR and VR systems is hardware compatibility and performance. AR and VR devices rely on a combination of sensors, cameras, displays, processors, and tracking systems to deliver immersive experiences to users. However, variations in hardware specifications, form factors, and performance capabilities among different devices can lead to compatibility issues, performance bottlenecks, and suboptimal experiences. Resolving hardware-related issues in AR and VR systems requires testing and validation across a range of devices, optimizing performance parameters, and implementing device-specific optimizations to ensure smooth and responsive experiences across diverse hardware ecosystems. Additionally, troubleshooting software compatibility issues is a common challenge in AR and VR systems, as these immersive experiences often rely on specialized software platforms, development frameworks, and content creation tools. Software compatibility issues may arise from incompatibilities between different versions of operating systems, runtime environments, graphics drivers, or software libraries used in AR and VR applications. Resolving software compatibility issues requires rigorous testing, debugging, and optimization of software components, ensuring compatibility with target platforms, and addressing any dependencies or runtime conflicts that may impact application performance or stability. Furthermore, optimizing user interface design and interaction mechanics is crucial for delivering intuitive and immersive experiences in AR and VR systems. User interface design in AR and VR environments differs significantly from traditional 2D interfaces, requiring considerations for spatial interaction, depth perception, gestural input, and immersive storytelling. However, designing effective user interfaces for AR and VR applications poses unique challenges, such as maintaining usability, minimizing cognitive load, and ensuring accessibility for diverse user populations. Resolving user interface design issues in AR and VR systems involves iterative prototyping, user testing, and usability evaluations to identify usability issues, refine interaction patterns, and optimize user experiences for enhanced immersion and engagement. Content creation and curation present another set of challenges in AR and VR systems, as creating compelling and immersive content requires specialized skills, tools, and techniques. Content creators must navigate the complexities of 3D modeling, animation, spatial audio, and interactive storytelling to deliver engaging experiences that captivate and delight users. However, content creation workflows in AR and VR environments can be time-consuming, resource-intensive, and technically demanding, requiring expertise in 3D graphics, animation, sound design, and narrative storytelling. Resolving content creation challenges in AR and VR systems involves providing creators with accessible tools, training resources, and collaborative platforms that streamline the content creation process, lower barriers to entry, and foster creativity and innovation. Moreover, optimizing performance and scalability is essential for delivering seamless and immersive experiences in AR and VR systems, especially in resource-constrained environments such as mobile devices or web browsers. Performance optimization involves maximizing frame rates, reducing latency, and minimizing rendering artifacts to ensure smooth and responsive interactions in AR and VR applications. Scalability optimization involves adapting content and experiences to different devices, screen sizes, and performance profiles while maintaining visual fidelity and immersion. Resolving performance and scalability issues in AR and VR systems requires profiling, tuning, and optimizing various aspects of the rendering pipeline, including geometry processing, texture mapping, shading, and post-processing effects. Additionally, addressing user discomfort and motion sickness is a critical challenge in AR and VR systems, as prolonged use of immersive technologies can cause discomfort, fatigue, or nausea in some users. Motion sickness in AR and VR environments is often attributed to factors such as inconsistent frame rates, latency, vection illusions, or mismatches between visual and vestibular cues. Resolving motion sickness issues in AR and VR systems involves implementing comfort features, such as smooth locomotion, field-of-view restrictions, and motion blur effects, as well as educating users about best practices for minimizing discomfort and acclimating to immersive experiences gradually. In summary, resolving issues in AR and VR systems requires a multidisciplinary approach that addresses hardware, software, design, content, performance, and user experience considerations. By leveraging a combination of technical expertise, creative innovation, and user-centric design principles, developers, designers, and content creators can overcome challenges and unlock the full potential of AR and VR technologies to create immersive, engaging, and impactful experiences for users across diverse domains and industries.

Chapter 10: Innovations in Troubleshooting Methodologies

Applying Agile troubleshooting principles involves adopting a dynamic and iterative approach to problem-solving that emphasizes collaboration, adaptability, and continuous improvement. Derived from Agile software development methodologies, Agile troubleshooting principles are increasingly being applied in various domains and industries to address complex and evolving technical challenges effectively. At the core of Agile troubleshooting is the principle of responsiveness, which emphasizes the importance of quickly identifying, prioritizing, and resolving issues to minimize downtime and mitigate impact on users or stakeholders. Agile troubleshooting teams prioritize customer satisfaction and value delivery by focusing on the most critical issues first and continuously refining their processes and practices to improve efficiency and effectiveness. One of the key principles of Agile troubleshooting is iterative problem-solving, which involves breaking down complex problems into smaller, manageable tasks or iterations that can be addressed incrementally. By tackling problems in small, bite-sized chunks, Agile troubleshooting teams can make steady progress, gather feedback early and often, and adapt their approach based on emerging insights and changing priorities. Another fundamental principle of Agile troubleshooting is collaboration, which emphasizes the importance of cross-functional teamwork and communication in identifying, analyzing, and resolving issues effectively. Agile troubleshooting teams bring together individuals with diverse skills, perspectives, and expertise to leverage collective intelligence, share knowledge, and foster innovation in problem-solving. By collaborating closely with stakeholders, subject matter experts, and end-users, Agile troubleshooting teams can gain deeper insights into the root causes of issues, explore alternative solutions, and make informed decisions that drive meaningful outcomes. Transparency is another core principle of Agile troubleshooting, which emphasizes open and honest communication, visibility into work progress, and shared understanding of goals, priorities, and challenges. Agile troubleshooting teams maintain transparent communication channels, such as daily stand-up meetings, Kanban boards, and issue tracking systems, to keep everyone informed, aligned, and engaged in the troubleshooting process. By fostering transparency, Agile troubleshooting teams can build trust, foster accountability, and empower individuals to take ownership of their work and contribute to collective problem-solving efforts. Adaptability is another critical principle of Agile troubleshooting, which emphasizes the ability to respond quickly and effectively to changing circumstances, unexpected challenges, and new information. Agile troubleshooting teams embrace change as a natural part of the problem-solving process, continuously reassessing priorities, adjusting strategies, and experimenting with new approaches to overcome obstacles and achieve their objectives. By embracing adaptability, Agile troubleshooting teams can remain resilient in the face of uncertainty, learn from failures, and capitalize on opportunities for innovation and improvement. Continuous improvement is the final principle of Agile troubleshooting, which emphasizes the importance of reflecting on past experiences, learning from mistakes, and refining processes and practices to enhance performance and outcomes over time. Agile troubleshooting teams regularly conduct retrospective meetings to review their work, identify areas for improvement, and implement action plans to address deficiencies and capitalize on successes. By fostering a culture of continuous learning and improvement, Agile troubleshooting teams can cultivate resilience, creativity, and excellence in problem-solving, driving long-term success and sustainability. In summary, applying Agile troubleshooting principles involves embracing responsiveness, iterative problem-solving, collaboration, transparency, adaptability, and continuous improvement to address complex technical challenges effectively. By adopting an Agile mindset and leveraging Agile practices and techniques, troubleshooting teams can enhance their effectiveness, efficiency, and impact in delivering value to customers, stakeholders, and end-users across diverse domains and industries.

Leveraging data analytics for troubleshooting optimization involves harnessing the power of data-driven insights and analytical techniques to enhance the efficiency, effectiveness, and accuracy of troubleshooting processes. In today's increasingly complex and interconnected IT environments, organizations face a myriad of technical challenges and issues that can impact system performance, reliability, and availability. By leveraging data analytics, organizations can gain deeper visibility into their IT infrastructure, identify patterns, trends, and anomalies, and make informed decisions to proactively prevent or quickly resolve issues before they escalate. At the heart of leveraging data analytics for troubleshooting optimization is the ability to collect, store, and analyze vast amounts of operational data generated by IT systems, applications, networks, and devices in real-time. This data includes logs, events, metrics, performance indicators, configuration settings, and user interactions, among other sources, which provide valuable insights into the health, behavior, and performance of IT environments. By aggregating and correlating diverse sources of operational data, organizations can gain a holistic view of their IT landscape, identify potential issues or bottlenecks, and prioritize troubleshooting efforts based on business impact and urgency. One of the key benefits of leveraging data analytics for troubleshooting optimization is the ability to detect and diagnose issues more quickly and accurately. By applying advanced analytics techniques, such as anomaly detection, machine learning, and predictive analytics, organizations can automatically identify deviations from normal behavior, detect potential anomalies or outliers, and alert IT teams to investigate and remediate issues proactively. For example, anomaly detection algorithms can analyze patterns in system logs, network traffic, or application performance metrics to identify unusual behaviors or deviations from established baselines that may indicate security incidents, performance degradation, or configuration errors. By detecting anomalies early, organizations can take timely corrective actions to prevent service disruptions, data breaches, or other adverse impacts on business operations. Furthermore, leveraging data analytics for troubleshooting optimization enables organizations to gain deeper insights into the root causes of issues and identify underlying systemic problems that may be contributing to recurring incidents or performance issues. By analyzing historical data and correlating events across different layers of the IT stack, organizations can uncover hidden dependencies, understand the impact of changes or configurations, and diagnose complex issues that span multiple systems or components. For example, root cause analysis techniques, such as fault tree analysis or causal inference models, can help IT teams trace the origins of incidents, identify contributing factors, and prioritize remediation actions to address underlying issues systematically. By addressing root causes, rather than just symptoms, organizations can prevent recurring incidents, improve system reliability, and enhance overall service quality. Another benefit of leveraging data analytics for troubleshooting optimization is the ability to automate repetitive or manual tasks, streamline workflows, and increase operational efficiency. By integrating data analytics tools and platforms with IT management systems, ticketing systems, and automation frameworks, organizations *can automate routine tasks, such as log analysis, event correlation, or incident triage, and focus human efforts on more strategic activities that require domain expertise or creative problem-solving skills. For example, automated incident response workflows can use predefined rules or machine learning models to classify and prioritize incoming alerts, assign them to appropriate teams or individuals, and suggest remediation actions based on historical patterns or best practices. By reducing manual intervention and accelerating response times, organizations can minimize downtime, improve service levels, and enhance customer satisfaction. Furthermore, leveraging data analytics for troubleshooting optimization enables organizations to proactively identify opportunities for performance optimization, capacity planning, and resource allocation. By analyzing historical data and trends, organizations can forecast future demand, anticipate potential scalability issues, and make data-driven decisions to optimize resource utilization, mitigate risks, and ensure service continuity. For example, capacity planning models can analyze workload patterns, resource utilization metrics, and performance trends to recommend optimal configurations, scaling policies, or infrastructure investments that align with business objectives and service level agreements. By optimizing resource allocation and scaling strategies, organizations can improve cost efficiency, maximize ROI, and deliver better value to customers and stakeholders. In summary, leveraging data analytics for troubleshooting optimization offers numerous benefits, including improved incident detection and diagnosis, deeper insights into root causes, automation of repetitive tasks, proactive performance optimization, and enhanced operational efficiency. By harnessing the power of data analytics, organizations can transform their troubleshooting processes, accelerate problem resolution, and deliver superior IT services that meet the evolving needs of their business and customers.*

Conclusion

In closing, the "IT Troubleshooting Skills Training" book bundle serves as a comprehensive and practical guide for analysts and managers seeking to enhance their problem-solving capabilities in the dynamic field of IT. Beginning with "Foundations of IT Troubleshooting: A Beginner's Guide," readers are equipped with fundamental concepts and techniques essential for navigating the complexities of IT systems and components. Moving on to "Mastering Common IT Issues: Intermediate Troubleshooting Techniques," individuals deepen their understanding and hone their skills in addressing prevalent challenges encountered in IT environments.

With "Advanced IT Problem-Solving Strategies: Expert-Level Troubleshooting," readers embark on a journey toward mastery, delving into sophisticated methodologies and approaches to tackle complex issues with precision and proficiency. Finally, "Beyond the Basics: Specialized Approaches in IT Troubleshooting" elevates the discourse by exploring specialized domains and cutting-edge strategies, empowering professionals to navigate the forefront of IT troubleshooting with confidence and agility.

Through these meticulously crafted volumes, readers are equipped with a robust toolkit encompassing foundational principles, intermediate techniques, expert strategies, and specialized approaches, enabling them to overcome a wide array of IT challenges effectively. Whether you're a novice seeking to build a strong foundation or a seasoned professional aiming to refine your expertise, this book bundle provides invaluable insights, practical guidance, and real-world examples to empower you on your journey toward becoming a proficient and resourceful troubleshooter in the ever-evolving landscape of IT.

www.ingramcontent.com/pod-product-compliance
Lightning Source LLC
Chambersburg PA
CBHW071235050326
40690CB00011B/2120